PHONICS, SPELLING, AND WORD STUDY:
A SENSIBLE APPROACH

Phonics, Spelling, and Word Study: A Sensible Approach

Susan Mandel Glazer
Rider University

Christopher-Gordon Publishers, Inc.
Norwood, Massachusetts

Credits

The Bill Harp Professional Teacher's Library
An Imprint of
Christopher-Gordon Publishers, Inc.
1502 Providence Highway, Suite #12
Norwood, MA 02062
(800) 934-8322

Printed in the United States of America

10 9 8 7 6 5 4 3 2 1   02 01 00 99 98

Library of Congress Catalog Card Number:
ISBN: 0-926842-82-X

Dedication

For the children who taught me about phonics and spelling,
for my early years teachers who saw potential anyway,
and
for Gail Turner who always gives me a word card.

Acknowledgements

The haste with which this book was assembled in order to make it available to you required cooperation from several people. These good folks are;

Phyllis Fantauzzo for Appendix A, the literature, and children's samples;

Katrin Kaja-Rooman for assembling the references;

Gail Turner for proofreading, managing, and mailing the manuscript.

A special thank you to **Ashley Edwards** for sharing her ability to self-monitor.

I could not have done it without you all.

CONTENTS

INTRODUCTION

'The politics of phonics, and beginning reading is like the flu; you don't like it but you know it has to take its course. The desire to stay out of the politics of teaching or not teaching phonics is due to what I refer to as the "phonics flu." Like the disease, the issues are seasonal, unreasonable, and generally destructive to children. The destructive aspects include the polarization of camps—the phonics folks versus those who don't do it. The bickering and feuding have minimal, short-term effects on the lives of adults engaged in these activities. It is the children who lose. Time, energy, and lack of attention to individual differences are sacrificed for the argument. Instead of fighting over "what" and "what not" to teach, we ought to be discovering ways to help each child learn to read and write. Instead of dealing with congressional bills and state mandates concerning "what" to teach, educators and parents ought to be concerned about finding as many ways as possible to guide individual children to using the coding system necessary to be literate.

This concise book shares several sensible, logical, and meaningful approaches that guide youngsters to use the written coding system to read, spell, and make meaning of our English language coding system. The book demonstrates that phonics, spelling, and word study are essential parts of literacy learning. One cannot read or write without the skills. The importance of these skills, however, must be put in proper perspective. There would be no coding system without phonics, spelling, and word study. But without content—the social studies, science, literature, art, and more—there would be no need for it.

SMG

CHAPTER 1

The History, The Strife, and The Charge For Change

Should Phonics and Spelling be Taught in School?

Of course phonics and spelling should be taught! Good teachers know children, especially during beginning stages, must have knowledge of the sound-symbol relationships in order to be successful readers and writers. Whether to teach or not to teach phonics is not the issue. The question really is, "How much positive press do we need to keep the populations of parents and politicians from flaring up again about the teaching of phonics?" This superficial, truly irresponsible question and answer is written half in jest, but not really. History justifies our concerns for public perceptions of the teaching of phonics, of all literacy activities.

Why Should We Be Concerned With Public Perceptions of the Teaching of Reading?

All of us are political. "But," as Morton Botel said to me once, "There's good politics, Susan, and bad." Teaching children to read has always, and will continue to be, both good and bad politics. For every stand there is to take, there are people to represent each. Politicians have used reading achievement as a campaign issue. Miss Americas and highly paid athletes take reading as their platform. First Ladies, heads of state, even theatrical folks are filmed reading to children, thus evoking good Samaritan sentiments from both friend and foe. We keep teaching children to read, in spite of laypersons who, because they are able to read, believe they can teach it. We keep our spirits up, and belief in children high even though we, the teachers, are the recipients of political and parental accusations that we have failed to make children literate.

Educators, especially classroom teachers, have accepted public displays of discontent with our professional activities. I am angry, and infuriated with the situation, and with us—the educators. We often sit back and accept criticism from people, most of whom who have no formal academic background in either the art or science of teaching and learning. I am embarrassed, too, when I discover educators who are unfamiliar with research illustrating effective ways for coaching a child into reading and writing.

So What?

What we need to do is know about language, its sounds, meanings, and rules, and how these interact simultaneously in reading and writing processes. Then we need to understand how our children learn. What's more, it is our responsibility to "politic" to convince the public that children are unique and different and that each learns differently, as well. Although parents accept differences in learning to read, most say, "But she has to learn phonics first!" Finally, it is my responsibility as teacher educator to provide you with information—the research, theories, and practices—you can use to support your instruction. And that's why I've written this book. It includes a brief history, theory, and practices that are sensible, and sensitive to children's uniquenesses. But, the writing hasn't been easy. The topic has caused me to move through more than the usual series of procrastinating rituals before beginning and the reason is quite clear: How to teach aspects of language including (1) phonics, (2) spelling, and (3) word study, phonics particularly, has caused strife and anxiety for millions of good teachers.

Phonics

The study of language has many aspects, but phonics is discussed the most. To paraphrase Hamlet, "To phonic or not to phonic, that is the question."

As a young teacher of very young children, I struggled with explicit phonics instruction. I knew, even three decades ago, there were political undertones to phonics instruction and, I'd "better" do it. I discovered that some children know that phonics was supposed to help them learn to read, but most didn't understand how. The children had a difficult time connecting explicit phonics instruction to word meaning. So, I found ways to incorporate the teaching of phonics through content area and literature studies, play and recreational activities. We studied phonics (phonemic awareness) in a scientific way, got data about the sounds of language, and assessed the idiosyncrasies. The children used the school district's adopted phonics series that I was told to use, but not in the way prescribed by the authors. The required weekly lesson plans were submitted to the principal in a traditional format, however. I knew I had to disguise my classroom activities, or I'd be reprimanded. Since the activities were successful for more children, I continued to use them. Many of the children found ways to understand how sounds and symbols are used to facilitate the decoding process. So, I continued to camouflage lesson plans so that they appeared like those expected for phonics instruction.

Years of experience have taught me that there is no one way for children to learn. There is also no way to separate phonics from reading, or even to take it away. Astuteness cultivated through the years has guided me to understand that public figures have used phonics as a tool for gaining notoriety.

I've attempted, in this chapter, to provide ideas for teaching and testing phonemic awareness and analysis, spelling, and word study in healthy, productive ways. There are ideas for those of you who believe that implicit instruction is the way. There are also ideas for teachers who believe that explicit, teacher-directed instruction is most effective.

What Is Phonics?

Phonics, says Sandra Wilde (1997), is the relationship between the sounds of language and the letters used to represent them. Phonics, in classrooms, is instruction that guides children to decode words using these relationships, in order to learn to read. Many agree that, in order to read and also write successfully, learners must be aware of sound/symbol relationships. Understanding the principles of our coding system (the alphabet) is important in the reading/ writing process, as well.

What's Important?

There are two distinct areas of instruction important for success in reading and writing: (1) phonemic and morphemic awareness, and spelling and, (2) increased vocabulary for reading and writing. Understanding the meanings of words and how to use them in appropriate contexts is essential for both good readers and writers. What and how to teach children to spell and decode words, and how to guide children to increase their knowledge of word meanings continues to be controversial. Most argue about the importance of learning to decode words using a phonics approach. Still others debate how much phonics instruction is needed. These aspects of language study have been at the root of the continuous debate—how to teach our children to read.

Why Controversies?

The belief that phonics instruction is THE most important variable for teaching beginning and unsuccessful learners to read has distorted the public's understanding of the reading/writing process. Even quality research in the area of phonics has often been misinterpreted to please the public, which seems to want to hear that "phonics works." In addition, education concerning the history of the English language is rare in professional development activities. Lack of knowledge about how we can craft American English, with all of its glitches and idiosyncrasies, results in inappropriate instruction about how language works to make words and their meanings.

Phonics, Phonemic Awareness, and Reading and Writing

The predictable resurgence of the notion that phonics is the key to success in reading has detracted the public from considering other important aspects of language and learning to read. I agree with many (Perfetti & Zhang, 1996; Routman, 1996) that phonics is important for children to learn. But the focus on phonological skills has "over-blown" its importance for success in reading and writing. Even children, when asked what they do when they don't know a word, respond, "I sound it out." Although there are many strategies for decoding words, "sounding out" and "asking someone" seem to be the two known to most children and adults (Routman, 1996).

Reading tests assessing phonics skills are, in part, responsible for the "over-blown" importance of phonics, especially when scores are low. The sounds become the important content, exaggerating their role in the reading process. The quiet, unnatural environment in which children usually take these tests casts a spell of caution for youngsters, for these times feel very different than instructional sessions.

This exaggerated thinking about reading instruction is not new. So much media "hype" existed in the early 1950s about reading instruction that the United States Office of Education (USOE) launched a study involving twenty-seven individual projects whose goal was comparing and contrasting the effectiveness of alternative approaches to teaching beginning reading. According to the findings, approaches that in one way or another included systematic phonics instruction consistently exceeded the straight basal program in word recognition achievement scores. The approaches that included both systematic phonics and considerable emphasis on connecting reading and meaning surpassed the basal-alone approaches on virtually all measures. In addition, the data indicated that exercises in writing were an important component of beginning reading instruction (Bond & Dykstra, 1967). The notorious volume *Becoming a Nation of Readers* (1985) includes a summary of research concerning early phonics indicating that children who had received intensive phonics instruction in kindergarten or first grade performed better in the third grade than a comparison group of children on both a word identification test and a comprehension test. By the sixth grade, the group that years earlier had received intensive phonics instruction still did better than the comparison group on a word identification test. However, the advantage in comprehension had disappeared. The fact that an early phonics emphasis had less influence on comprehension as the years passed is probably attributed to the increasing importance of knowledge of the topic, vocabulary, and reasoning ability on advanced comprehension tests. Follow up research in the 1970s suggests that instructional models emphasizing basic skills (phonics) tended to elicit the best achievement scores, especially in the first and second grades. Evaluations were weaker in third grade as well as fourth (Becker & Gersten, 1982). This occurred because of the shift from decoding to comprehension needs as children progress upward in the grades.

Editors Readence and Barone's (1997) insightful reprinting of the first grade studies reflects their keen insight into history's lessons. Their sensitivity to the past, coupled with their insights into the current resurgence of interest in phonics, had to be an impetus for the marvelous issue of *Reading Research Quarterly, 32* (4).

Conclusions from scholarly works indicate that phonics instruction is important for many children in the early grades. I, as well as others (Perfetti & Zhang, 1996), agree that the ability to understand phonological (the sound system) concepts associated with our language is important for reading. When children can identify words and say them, comprehension improves, especially when word identification is quick and automatic (Perfetti, 1992). Even skilled readers sound out words they don't recognize. They recode printed words into the sounds they represent so effortlessly and automatically that they don't realize it's happening (Tannenhaus, Flanigan, & Seidenberg, 1980).

Often skilled readers recognize words by taking "sophisticated guesses" (Adams, 1991). This occurs when there is information about how words are spelled in the readers' memories. Skilled readers have acquired the ability to scan words, identifying them without attending to every detail (Adams, 1991). The automaticity with which they are able to do this results because written English is redundant, and often predictable. When, for example, you see the letter **"q"** you will predict that it is followed by a **"u."** When you see a **"z, h, or y"** you take a sophisticated guess, predicting that a vowel most probably comes next. You've learned, from interacting with the language, that **sl** is a letter combination that starts words, but **ls** is not.

Phonemic awareness is more than knowledge about sounds. It requires one to have a well-developed visual memory, which increases one's ability to use phonics and spelling correctly. Children need to be able to picture letters and words and hold these in their memories.

Even when phonemic and visual memory skills are well developed, youngsters may still have problems. The fact that there are twenty-six letters and some don't represent the sounds of the language in consistent ways is usually the cause. It was George Bernard Shaw who said that the word *fish* might as well be spelled *ghoti*—*gh* as in *rough,* *o* as in *women,* and *ti* as in *vacation.* New young writers spell fish **FS, FES, FESHE** and sometimes **FX,** but never **GHOTI.** The children's spellings and also Mr. Shaw's are both incorrect, confirming the fact that matching letters with sounds can have several results. Mr. Shaw's extensive experience with the sounds of language justifies his creative spellings.

Understanding sound-symbol relationships is important, but it is not enough. Learners must also be able to expand their vocabulary and knowledge about the English language. Information about the derivations of the American English language, and how language works, improves comprehension. We need to know the foibles of the English language and what causes them.

The Study and Foibles of the English Language

Some historical knowledge about the American English language helps to explain why aspects of the language can be confusing. The history puts the importance of phonics in a more realistic perspective.

English reflects the various languages from which it has been derived. We have been scavengers, borrowing words from languages including German, Danish, Norman French, Church Latin, Classical Latin, and Greek (Henderson, 1985). We've also taken words from Arabia, India, the Americas—both native and Spanish, Polynesia, Russia, and even Tibet. These have been absorbed into American English in order to have the words necessary to communicate effectively. Ralph Waldo Emerson once defined English as "the sea which receives tributaries from every region under heaven" (McCrum, Cran, & MacNeil, 1992, p. 1). The inclusive *Oxford English Dictionary* lists over 500,000 words and an additional half-million technical and scientific terms. German has about 185,000 words and French fewer than 100,000. Of the world's approximately 2,700 languages, English is the richest in vocabulary (McCrum, Cran, & MacNeil, 1992).

The amazing thing about English is how the language has spread. Over the past one hundred years, at least three to four hundred million people have learned to speak it as a second language. English today is spoken by about 750 million people. Three-quarters of the world's mail, telexes, and cables are in English, and so are half the world's technical and scientific periodicals (McCrum, Cran, & MacNeil, 1992). It is the official voice of the air and sea, and 80 percent of the information stored in the world's computers is in English (McCrum, Cran, & MacNeil, 1992).

A Very Brief History of English

English did not exist when Julius Caesar landed in Britain a little over 2,000 years ago (McCrum, Cran, & MacNeil, 1992). When first used 500 years later, it was incomprehensible to most and spoken by only a few.

Old English (600 to 1100 A.D.)

The earliest spoken form of English, referred to as Old or Saxon English, emerged between 500 A.D. and 600 A.D. and continued until about 1100 A.D. Modern English, which is what we read and write today, evolved during the 1400 and 1500s.

The following points from the period of Old English seem important for teachers today.

1. English was the first of the modern European languages to attain a standard written form.

2. The written form was used for functional as well as artistic purposes.

3. English originally had a more regular spelling system with Latin letters (Baugh, 1983).

Old English was spelled the way the language sounds. New writers spell that way as exhibited by the sign written by a five-year-old.

B ki t i m rkeee.

(Translation: Be quiet I am working).

Middle English (1100 to 1500 A.D.)

Old English was an oral language. The need for a written code emerged with Middle English. Words dealing with social dress (**garment, attire**), law (**jury, evidence**), church (**religion, sermon**), arts and medicine (**painting, physician**), and government (**royal, mayor**) were words borrowed from French. Borrowed words altered English pronunciations, creating interesting, complex spellings. Words were often respelled from one language to another. Alterations from English to French forms such as **is** for **ice** and **mys** for **mice** caused confusion. Combinations of words from Latin and English resulted in replacing the vowel letter **u** with the letter **o**. Because **u** was used so often, the English adopted the French spelling **ou**, which is the reason for the spellings of the words **loud, through, wound,** and **soup.** Combining Anglo-Norman-English spelling led to different vowel sounds represented by the digraph **ea (ease, measure)** and to variations of the long **e,** as spelled in **piece, people,** and **meet.**

The merging of many oral and written conventions disrupted the relatively consistent relationship between the letters and the sounds used in Old English. When immigrant workers began to set type at the time the printing press was invented in the 1400s, their crude knowledge of English turned into curious spellings. Since spellings went unmonitored, spellings were printed and became part of the language. However, forces were at work altering the language so that it took the form of the modern English of Shakespeare, basically the language that is in use today (McCrum, Cran, & MacNeil, 1992).

From Middle to Modern English

Because of the communication demands of the information age, Latin and Greek words and spellings were melded to French and English. Within a hundred years, the pronunciation of English changed. This "great vowel shift" caused long vowels to change so that one vowel sound began to take the place of another. Long **a,** for example, originally pronounced **ah** as in **father,** became **a** as in **name. E** "stole" the old sound of long **i.** When young children try to guess what vowel letter to use for short **i,** as in **tin,** they choose **e** as in **ten.** They also spell **pet** as **pat** (Henderson, 1985). So, vowels were disjuncted from their normally paired relationships whose sounds were consistent. The time line in Figure 1-1 provides a terse overview of the critical points in the history of the English language.

Time, People, and Their Influence on the English Language	
Year	**Event**
55 B.C.	Julius Caesar attempts to conquer Britain and is unsuccessful.
50 A.D.	Celtic and Latin coexist when Claudius I colonizes Britain.
450	Teutonic tribes invade Britain and Romans leave.
600	Old English acquires written code when England divides.
750	The Danes invade England, bringing their language with them.
1066	Norman French becomes the language of the state when William of Normandy conquers England. English remains the language of the people.
1350	Middle English is made the official language of the English Parliament during the Hundred Years War (Edward III's reign).
1420	Middle English is first used in his correspondence by Henry V.
1476	English borrows words from classical languages of the Renaissance, and the first printing press is used.
1603	Modern English is used by Elizabeth I and William Shakespeare in their writings.
1755	First comprehensive dictionary is compiled by Samuel Johnson.
1828	Noah Webster compiles the first dictionary of American English.
(Henderson, 1985; McCrum, Cran, & MacNeil, 1992).	

Figure 1-1.   Dates of Events That Influenced the English Language.

The English language system was further confused by social and political issues, especially the concept that there are many "Englishes." There's the "Queen's" English, American English, dialects of American English, and Englishes spoken as a second language. The "Englishes" one speaks establishes who one is, and what one may become. I remember hearing a friend say, "Oh, he talks like he's had an Ivy League education." Humans see themselves as members of particular groups based on how they use language (F. Smith, 1995).

If you have come to the conclusion that modern English is dreadfully confusing, political, and complex, you are correct. Children, however, have learned to use English for centuries. This is possible because the system is complex, but not chaotic.

So, Who Should Learn Phonics, Spelling, and Aspects of Word Study?

How children acquire knowledge about letter-sound relationships, and how that knowledge is facilitated, is central in the development of word concepts (Perfetti, 1992). It is well known that many school failures are the result of inappropriate instructional procedures. How we guide children, therefore, to use strategies and the context in which skills are acquired makes a difference in what and how they learn.

Phonics, Morphemic Analysis, and Spelling: Understanding Sound-Symbol Relationships

Fred Fedorko, a colleague in our field, shared a story about a six-year-old who, when asked if he was going to fall in love replied, "No, I won't. If it's anything like phonics, I don't want to have anything to do with it." Well, for some children phonics is like falling in love with the wrong person. It just doesn't work. But for others it is wonderful. It's our job, as teachers, to make the decisions about the appropriateness of teaching and using phonics or anything else.

Children's needs must be assessed before instruction begins. I consider assessment part of the instructional process. So, assessment occurs while children are engaged in all activities. As chil-

Who CAN (Most Probably) Use Phonics

Phonics is probably appropriate when the child— Yes No Not sure

	Yes	No	Not sure
Picks out letters and says their names.	☐	☐	☐
Notices, without prompting, letter/sound matches.	☐	☐	☐
Rhymes easily.	☐	☐	☐
At times, confuses initial consonant sounds with rhyming. When asked, "Tell me another word that starts with 'r' like in 'rat,' may say, 'cat.'"	☐	☐	☐
Says "I know what letter it starts with" at an early age (older threes and four-year-olds) when long vowels and consonants appear at the beginning of words.	☐	☐	☐
Sometimes uses pictures to guide decoding of words.	☐	☐	☐
Creates her/his own logical spellings based on the sound-symbol relationships of our language.	☐	☐	☐
When writing, can be seen "sounding out" words.	☐	☐	☐
Attends to one letter in a word, when writing. Needs strategies for attending to others.	☐	☐	☐
Demonstrates confidence when "taking risks" and spelling words as they sound.	☐	☐	☐
Although they may not be correct, uses vowels in words illustrating an awareness of spelling conventions.	☐	☐	☐
Spellings seem to become conventional the more she/he writes.	☐	☐	☐
Rereads and self-corrects some spellings of words.	☐	☐	☐
Enjoys talking about how to make (spell) words.	☐	☐	☐

Figure 1-2.   Who CAN (Most Probably) Use Phonics?

dren read and write, listen, look, and record observations of their behaviors in order to determine each's propensities for using phonics. I've hesitated to create Figures 1-2 and 1-3, but they have been helpful (when used cautiously) for deciding who can and cannot use phonics as a word recognition tool.

Some children intuitively understand relationships between sounds and symbols. They rhyme words and play with sounds even in the toddler years. Some children—as early as three-and-a-half—write, matching letters with sounds. There are some whose ability to match letters and sounds are not as well developed, nor will they ever be. These children, no matter what activity is used, respond inappropriately or in unexpected ways to instructional approaches. These children are very often poor spellers in the

---

Who CANNOT (Most Probably) Use Phonics

Phonics is probably inappropriate when the child—   Yes   No   Not sure

	Yes	No	Not sure
Seems to be unable to make any sense of sound-symbol relationships.	☐	☐	☐
WILL NOT attempt to use word attack skills.	☐	☐	☐
Has difficulty pronouncing words accurately.	☐	☐	☐
Reverses letters at the age of 8, or older.	☐	☐	☐
Spells words as if they were spelled differently.	☐	☐	☐
Confuses consonant sounds.	☐	☐	☐
Uses physical more often than verbal expressions.	☐	☐	☐
Responds inconsistently to sounds.	☐	☐	☐
Handwriting is often illegible due to an inability to remember letter shapes.	☐	☐	☐
Has difficulty rhyming words.	☐	☐	☐
Can copy something almost perfectly, but without copying, writing is illegible.	☐	☐	☐

Figure 1-3.   Who CANNOT (Most Probably) Use Phonics

elementary grades, and even into high school and college. They're sometimes those "inbetweeners" who can make sense of some of the regularities and irregularities of the coding system, but find other aspects of the language difficult.

Children who have difficulty using phonics exhibit combinations of many of the behaviors described in Appendix B. REMEMBER, some of the characteristics are present in all of us. But children with difficulties exhibit many of them. Children with severe problems usually produce products (drawings, stories, etc.) that are significantly different from those of others in the classroom. Often, their excessive inability to remember stands out. Experiments with alternative strategies suggested for these students are included later in this book. If the youngster is still unsuccessful, and exhibits an excessive number of the characteristics included in Appendix B, seek guidance from a reading specialist, school psychologist, or other appropriate specialists.

Teaching and Assessing Phonemic and Morphemic Awareness, and Spelling

We've asked children to look at mismatches between letters and sounds—the irregularities. We ask them to understand about the coding system as if their experiences were numerous. For example, many teachers explain about letters and their sounds. They discuss these aspects in isolation. The sounds and letters become the content, rather than a tool for recognizing ideas. Children are expected to notice minimal sounds and visual contrasts between words including **bed** and **bad, tin** and **ten, went** and **want, farm** and **from.** If they use the oral code for something that is represented in print, confusion is even greater. When teachers tell without modeling the behaviors they expect of youngsters, children are often frightened away from examining language. Some are virtually paralyzed, causing them to memorize rather than decode words.

Many children have a natural affinity for phonics and spelling. Beginning writers exhibit this affinity with their crude, but nearly perfect phonetic correspondence between letter sounds and the symbols representing the sounds (see Figure 1-4). This natural (often referred to as "invented") spelling is wonderful, but can distort, even obliterate the basis for and meanings of many words. So, it makes sense to guide children to study the regular, reliable, and manageable sounds and meaning units of English, first.

Figure 1-4.

Although not supported by other research, we have found that approximately 900 children between the ages of five and eight have defined sounds of language during explicit instruction as summarized below (Glazer, 1980–1997). The explanations follow, for the most part, the alphabetic principles.

1. Some letter sounds say their names as long as your breath will last. These letters include all of the long vowels (**a** as in **ape; e** as in **eat; i** as in **ice; o** as in **ocean; u** as in **unicorn**).

2. Some letters do not say their names, but you can still hold onto the sounds as long as your breath lasts (**a-apple, e-egg, i-insect, o-octopus, u-umbrella, c-circus, f-fish, h-hot, l-love, m-mom, n-nurse, r-read, s-sun, v-vanilla, w-warm, z-zoo**).

3. You can figure out some sounds because of the way you say the letter names. These include the long vowels (see #1 above) and also **b** as in **ball, c-circus, d-dad, f-food, g-giraffe, h-hello, j-jelly, k-kite, l-lamb, m-milk, n-noodle, p-puppy, q-quack, r-ring, s-snake, t-tiger, v-violin, x-x-ray,** and **z** as in **zebra**.

4. Some letters have more than one sound. These are **c** sounds like **k** in **cake, s** in **is** borrows the sound from **c** in **circle,** soft **g** borrows the sound from **j** as in **giraffe, s** sounds like **c** in **facade, y** as in **yes** or as in **happy.**

The collection of childrens' comments are practical, sensible, and easy to understand. It's clear that talk about language and games that instigate cognitive awareness guide all children to become phonemically aware.

Summary

Controversies continue, debates ensue, and we continue to teach. History has taken its toll on our language and the consequences of growth prevail. If we had not emigrated and met others who had done the same, the English language would be as phonemically regular as the natural spellings of beginning writers. So, we must take a clue from history and respect the changes, and take responsibility for informing laypersons of the reasons why some children learn with phonics and others do not. There are, however, strategies to guide ALL children to understand that there are unique ways to make words, decode them, and remember how to spell them. The children must know what these are.

Things To Think About

1. What, from your experiences, do you believe are the reasons for the public's intense interest in the teaching of reading and writing?

2. Make a list of all of the things you know about the sound-symbol relationships of the English language.

3. Make a list of all of the things about the sound-symbol relationships that are confusing.

CHAPTER 2

 Teaching Phonics

There are no definitive answers, formulas, or commercial programs that "teach" phonics. There is no one program to cure the ills of beginning readers, either. So, the continuous controversies over the order and method for teaching the sounds of language continues. But, they ought to stop. We must think of the children, compromise for their sake and their parents, and consider both (1) implicit (integrated or indirect) and, (2) explicit (direct) instruction. We need to begin by realizing that quality instructional outcomes result in students questioning themselves about issues. The self-questioning is self-assessment and also instruction. The process of self-assessment is ongoing. A person asks himself questions then searches for data to support an answer. Students "flip-flop" back and forth between the two. They ask questions about their accomplishments—that's the assessment. Then they collect data and answer the questions. Especially when instruction is implicit—that is, when it happens within the context of content areas—assessment must also be implicit. Figures 1-2 and 1-3 (pages 12 and 13) are guides for observing each child's readiness for phonological instruction. I suggest that you concentrate on observing two children at a time. I also suggest that you notice the child carrying out these behaviors at least three times, in several different activities, in order to make a judgment concerning readiness.

Although traditional testing approaches are less desirable for assessing readiness, use them if you must (for whatever reason), to determine readiness. If you do, you need to create role-play situations prior to administering the tests that replicate the test-taking experience. The children will become familiar with the testing environment, and will be less stressed during testing.

Assess children's ability to use aspects of phonics. Continuously "listen and look" at each child's behaviors. When you hear or see children using each phonic skill at least three times daily in functional settings, they own those skills. Describe their interactions with and knowledge about phonemes by using the descriptors in Figures 2-1, 2-2, 2-3, 2-4, and 2-5 Review children's products—things they write—to notice the following:

- when "natural" (invented) spellings reflect the sounds;.
- when children talk frequently about sounds and are correct.*

Assessing Awareness of Sound/Symbol Relationships			
Description of Behavior	Yes	No	Needs more practice
Knows letter names, and identifies them, in lower and upper case formats.	☐	☐	☐
Points to letters, says their names without prompts.	☐	☐	☐
Rhymes words in conversations without request.	☐	☐	☐
When writing, attempts to sound letters for writing. May say "p-p-p-p-p-p-pap-p-p-per," for example.	☐	☐	☐
Talks about the sounds of letters (i.e., "This is an e, see! It says eeeeeeeeeee.").	☐	☐	☐

Figure 2-1.   Assessing Awareness of Sound/Symbol Relationships

---

* The following was used to identify phonic elements. Develop additional observation guides that include other phonic elements using this helpful resource— Fry, E., Kress, J., & Fountoukidis, D. (Eds.) (1993). *The Reading Teacher's Book of Lists.* New York: The Center for Applied Research.

Listen, Look, and Assess Knowledge About Phonics

Analyzing Sounds of Words: Phonics	Yes	No	Not sure

Recognizes single letters that say their names as long as their breath lasts and makes the correct sound or writes the correct symbol representing the sounds. ☐ ☐ ☐

These include:
a as in ape, **e** as in eat, **i** as in ice, **o** as in open, **u** as in uniform.

Recognizes and makes or writes the sound/symbols for letters that do not say their names but you can still hold onto the sound as long as your breath lasts. These include some letters whose sounds you can figure out by the way you say the letter name (see the next item). ☐ ☐ ☐

These include:
a as in apple, **e** as in egg, **i** as in insect, **o** as in octopus, **u** as in umbrella, **c** as in circus, **f** as in fish, **h** as in hot, **l** as in love, **m** as in mom, **n** as in nurse, **r** as in red, **s** as in sister, **v** as in vampire, **w** as in wash, **z** as in zebra.

Figures out the sound because of the way you say the letter name.

These include:
b as in boy, **c** as in circle, **d** as in dad, **f** as in fairy, **j** as in jelly, **k** as in kite, **l** as in lamb, **m** as in mitten, **n** as in nest, **p** as in potato, **q** as in quiet, **r** as in rooster, **s** as in sneaker, **t** as in toast, **v** as in violin, **x** as in x-ray, and **z** as in zipper.

Recognizes some letters have more than one sound because they borrow sounds from other letters. ☐ ☐ ☐

These are:
c as in cake, and **c** as in circus; **g** as in giraffe, and **g** as in gadget; **y** as in yes, **y** as in happy.

Figure 2-2. Listen, Look, and Assess Knowledge About Phonics

Consonant Blends

Directions: Observe children's unguided written products. Notice their use of each consonant blend. Include children's spellings on appropriate line. Prepare instruction for those who seem to "have an idea" about a blend, but need guidance. When a child uses a blend three times without intervention, he/she has mastered that phonemic element.

r family blends

br _____

cr _____

dr _____

fr _____

gr _____

pr _____

tr _____

wr _____

l family blends

bl _____

cl _____

fl _____

gl _____

pl _____

sl _____

s family blends

sc _____

sk _____

sm _____

sn _____

sp _____

st _____

sw _____

no family

tw _____

3 letter blends

scr _____

squ _____

str _____

thr _____

spr _____

spl _____

shr _____

sch _____

Figure 2-3.   Consonant Blends

Consonant Digraphs, Exceptions, Rare Exceptions, and Silent Consonants

Directions: Observe children's writing. Listen and look as they speak. Notice if oral pronunciation and writing match (writing represents the way the child says phonemes).

Consonant Digraphs: beginning & endings of words

ch _____

sh _____

th (voiced) _____

th (voiceless) _____

wh (hw blend) _____

Rare Exceptions

ch = /k/ as in "character"

_____

ch = /s/ as in "chef"

_____

ti = /sh/ as in "attention"

_____

s = /sh/ as in "sure"

_____

x = /gz/ as in "exact"

_____

Exceptions

qu = /kw/ as in "quick"

_____

ph = /f/ as in "phone"

_____

c = /s/ before i, e, y, as in "city"

_____

c = /k/ before a, o, u, as in "cap" _____

g = /g/ before i, e, y, as in "gem" _____

g = /g/ before a, o, u, as in "good" _____

x = /ks/ as in "vex" _____

s = /z/ at end of some words as in "is" _____

Silent Consonants

gn = /n/ as in "gnat" _____

kn = /n/ as in "knife" _____

wr = /r/ as in "write" _____

Student demonstrates knowledge about phonics to create the following words: _____

_____

Figure 2–4.   Consonant Digraphs, Exceptions, Rare Exceptions, and Silent Consonants

Recognizing Two-Letter Combinations

Directions: Notice students' use of these in written products. If used three times incorrectly, provide explicit instruction. When used three times correctly, use of two-letter combination is probably learned.

a-e vowel sound	Other two-letter combinations
ate _____	**e** as in "hose" _____
final **e** as in "ace" _____	**ai** as in "rain" _____
final **e** as in "life" _____	**au** as in "author" _____
	ar as in "stare" _____
	ar as in "start" _____
	ee as in "see" _____
	ea as in "seat" _____
	ea as in "dead" _____
	er as in "her" _____
	ng as in "sing" _____
	oa as in "coat" _____
	or as in "ore" _____
	ow as in "cow" _____
	oy as in "toy" _____
	oi as in "coil" _____
	ou as in "out" _____
	oo as in "look" _____
	oo as in "zoo" _____

Student uses knowledge represented above and creates the following words: _____

_____

Figure 2-5.   Recognizing Two-Letter Combinations

Make a photocopy of Figures 1-2, and 2-1 through 2-5 for each child. Use them to guide your observations of children's phonemic awareness as well as knowledge of letter sounds. Do not use these figures to create tests that require youngsters to select the "right answer." Use them when observing children as they write, read, and play phonic games. Check "yes" when the child uses a phonic element at least three times independently. Then you can be fairly sure that they have conceptualized the specific sounds of letters as they are used in words;

Implicit assessment—looking and listening within the context of all school activities—can also be used for determining children's ability to use and understand the following:

- consonant blends at the beginning and endings of words;
- consonant digraphs at beginnings and end of words **(ch, sh, th, wh)**;
- phonograms (usually a vowel sound plus a consonant sound). These are the families that make rhyming games fun. Some phonograms include **at**–as in **cat, all**–as in **tall, air**–as in **hair.**

Figure 2-2, 2-3, and 2-4 provide parameters for noticing children's competence with blends, diagraphs, and some phonograms.

Implicit Phonics Instruction

When children begin to notice and talk about language naturally, teachers and caregivers need to seize that moment of readiness,* and begin a discussion. When six-year-old Shana said, "Teacher, the poem has letters that all say the alphabet names," the child is indicating that it's time for instruction.

When the Opportunity Arises, Implicit Instruction

I recently overheard a four-year-old say to his mother, "Look," as he pointed to the sign above the counter in a physician's waiting room, "Look, Mommy. It has a **P** like my name." Peter's mother had

---

*"Readiness," usually used to describe the preparedness of children in the beginning school years, refers in this text to one's preparedness to cope with tasks at all ages.

been reading a magazine, but she seized the teachable moment, responding, "You are right, Pete. That word, **pay**, starts like Peter. Look," she said, pointing to a captioned picture in the magazine, "this is a picture of a picnic. See, here's **picnic**" (pointing to the word in the magazine). "This looks like a family, like ours, on a picnic. Picnic starts like Peter, too. And your sister's name, **Patty,** does too." On the car ride home, Peter and his mom played the game of finding all of the things that started with a "P" like his name. She coached the child, providing clues by making her lips into the formation used before saying, "Peter," and also naming many objects. Transactions between the mother and child illustrate the following:

Child's Behaviors	Mother's Behaviors	Interpretations
Notices and makes connection between what he knows (his name) and the environmental print.	Seizes the teachable moment, and provides additional examples of words that start like Pete's name.	Mother knows how to observe and notice child's need and readiness for a concept. Uses child's language as a starting point for instruction.
Demonstrates ability to match and describe the initial sound of "p" by providing a word that begins with "p."	Coaches by using body language to encourage the child to participate.	Teaches by contributing as a learner, so child will model her behavior.

In conversation with this mother, I learned that she and Peter played the game often. Peter usually began the game, and his mother followed. At times, Peter asked his mother to write words that were of personal interest to him. These included his name, Peter, and his sister's name, Patty. On one occasion he asked her to write Misty, his dog's name. The request was followed by, "I know it doesn't have a 'P'." The child provided data confirming that he understood how

"P" sounded. This is the ultimate test. The child was able to differentiate, without prompting, the sound of "P" in a real setting.

I recall hearing my nephews, nieces, and godchildren playing with language as toddlers. "La—dee, la—dee, la—dee" or other rhyming type words were repeated over and over again. As they grew, I had the pleasure of taking them on day trips. Once when walking, I began to say, "Billy silly, nilly, whilly, hilly." The three-year-old looked at me with a smile, as I repeated "Billy, silly." Then I paused, bent down next to him using body language that said, join me, and began again. "B-i-l-l-y, s-i-l-l-y," and he began with me, "ch-i-l-l-y, n-i-l-l-y," until we exhausted the "illy" word family.

Playing with Words

Rhyming books, poetry, and books with repeated language are adored by children. Authors like Dr. Seuss, Lee Bennett Hopkins, Paul Galdone, and others (see Appendix A) have written enticing poetry and story books using repetitive language. Spelling patterns (*at*, as in *fat, bat, cat,* etc.), repeated sentences (I'll huff and I'll puff and I'll blow your house down!), and rhyming words catch children's fascination, luring them to want to hear and produce more of the same. It's fun, when reading these to children, to leave out the rhyming word at the end of each sentence after they've heard that pattern several times. Children will partially participate, and automatically rhyme, saying the final word correctly.

Language plays—those tricky, sticky, lickity split oral and written language games—present language opportunities and also help children discover the complexities and fascinations of language. Jim Moffett (Moffett & Wagner, 1992) defined word play as the category of discourse that entices children most of all. They include tongue twisters, puns, word puzzles and games, pictographs and cryptograms, brain teasers, concrete and typographical poetry, light-hearted verse and songs in this category. We know about these wonderful "language plays" because of authors like Dr. Seuss, Lewis Carroll, Ogden Nash, and the lyricist and composer Tom Lehrer. There are so many plays with words and authors who created them. These fascinating language arrangements are referred to by students in our Center for Reading and Writing at Rider University as "stuff" that's just for fun (JFF). The examples included here thus far have been implicit in their instruction in phonics. They are immersed in the contexts of literature and poetry.

Explicit Instruction

The following activities are designed for those children who need or might like direct instruction. They receive support and comfort from small-group strategies. They also may need to hear about the aspects of language they may already know implicitly.

Language Play

Our youngsters call some language play JFF (**J**ust **F**or **F**un). The activities can serve as guides for creating more language plays and games in both formal and informal settings.

Tongue Twisters

Tongue twisters, such as *those **thrilling thermal thrashing thrilling thumping thin thesis,*** can be created with blends and digraphs that appear at the beginning or the ending of words. Any words that start or end with the same letter combinations lend themselves to JFF exercises. The following are examples.

Same Beginning, Different Ending

Snoring sneaky snails sniff snakes' sneakers.

Flying flags flank flowering floats.

Splashing splitting splatting splattering splinters splendidly splice splints.

Same Ending, Different Beginning

A bath and math wrath my path.

A slick quick thick chick named Rick tricked sick Nick.

A Model Lesson for ALL Phonic Skills

I like to use a learning model to create activities. Don Holdaway's (1979) four-step instructional model is one of my favorite frameworks. His four steps to learning—(1) observations of actions to be learned; (2) partial participation with a mentor who is engaged in the actions; (3) role-play or rehearsal independently; and (4) performance—the time to share with others the accomplishments—follow the learning model human beings use naturally from birth.

The following format for instruction can be used for all phonics instruction as well as other content learning.

Session #1.   Bombard Students with Correct Answers: Model So They Can Observe

1. Use the element (word family, blend, etc.) to be learned or as much as you naturally can in your oral language.

2. Find poems, tongue twisters, riddles, and jokes that use the element again and again. Read or tell them to children (more for children to observe).

3. Repeat, tell, or read the language plays, encouraging children to say the words that begin or end with the blend, digraph or other phoneme, encouraging partial participation.

4. Once children partially participate, create charts with the blend, digraph, initial or final consonants, etc., printed at the top. Write two or three words that include the phoneme or letter combination and post the sign. Be sure there is a marker nearby. This will serve as a tool for children to rehearse using elements.

5. Gather the children who need explicit instruction (not more than six at once) around the chart with the letters to be studied written at the top.

6. Repeat one of the stories, poems, riddles, or other language plays that include lots of words with the letters of focus.

7. Each time you say a word that uses the letter, write it on the chart. Underline or highlight the letters of focus.

8. When you finish repeating the language play and have written the words, ask the following questions, one at a time:

    What letters are at the top of the chart? Where else do you see these letters? Where else?

9. Then say, "Let's read the words together." After the words are read by the group, ask, in a tone of voice that implies that you

are repeating the same questions again and again, "What's the same about each word?" This step involves partial participation with students.

These questions sometimes guide children to attend to specific phonemic characteristics. I've rationalized the use of questions by fitting them into Holdaway's first step—things to observe. Children are being asked to look as you model behavior at the easel.

Session #2.   Partial Participation and Rehearsal

Until this point, you have been providing children with the correct answer. Now it is their turn to "partially participate" and contribute.

Begin by gathering children in front of a posted easel paper with the phonemic element being studied written, in large font, at the top of the paper. Say, "Watch what I am doing so you can tell me what I did." Write words, saying each one at a time. If the letters at the top were "sh," for example, I'd write four to seven words, matching my voice to the speed of writing, "shoe, shop, ship, shepherd," etc. As I was about to complete the last word, I'd say, "O.K., who has a word that begins like 'ship'?" Encourage children to contribute, but do not restrict them from spontaneously "calling out." When they do call out, say in a lighthearted, fun way, "Hold your horses, I'm writing as quickly as I can." When you're finished, post several charts around the room with the letter combination written at the top of blank sheet of paper. Casually, during work or play times, write a word on a chart. Encourage children to write words that belong, too. Some will copy yours, others may use a dictionary, or ask another child to suggest a word. The purpose of the activity is to get them to "feel" the experience of writing, categorizing the words appropriately. It is helpful, therefore, for reluctant learners to have words that include the phoneme posted around the classroom. This permits children to look for answers in their immediate environments.

Session #3.   Provide Choices: A Game to Assess Effects of Instruction

I'm not sure Dr. Holdaway would agree with using the next activity. I'm suggesting something rather unorthodox, and against my better professional judgment. But, it works to excite and invite children to participate in an activity. This is the time that we "sort of" test the children by creating a game. In this game, children select and match letters with pictures of objects whose names begin with that letter combination. I suggest that you do the following:

1. Create enough cards with the letter combination in focus for the number of children you want to play the game together. Young children do best in pairs. Eight-year-olds and older enjoy a foursome.

2. Collect pictures of objects whose names, for example, begin with those letters. Make cut-out letters, or the phonemic element being studied, for as many as there are pictures. If, for example, there are twenty pictures that include objects whose initial consonants are "cr," make twenty cards with "cr" written on them, one on each.

3. Cut as many pieces of tagboard as there are pictures into the same size rectangle. Cut tagboard for mounting the letters, as well.

4. Pair the children using one table or desk for each. Tell, while demonstrating, how to cut one picture at a time and paste it onto a piece of tagboard. Do it again, and ask the children to do it with you. Move at the children's pace.

5. Demonstrate, with a partner, how to match a picture with the letter(s) that represents the beginnings of each word.

Children will discuss what they are doing during the construction activity. Listen and look to hear what each knows about letter/ sound relationships. You will be assessing as they create materials. The game insists children make correct responses, for all objects begin with the letters of focus.

Session #4.   Children Become Teachers and Create and Share

This is the fun part for children. They become teachers, sharing and bragging about their accomplishments. It usually happens when a child says, "Ms. Susan, look what I did!" Several ways to increase children's excitement while building vocabulary include:

- making a personal dictionary;
- making individual word charts with each youngster;
- writing words on cards and creating a personal word wallet;
- cutting words that include the letters studied from newspapers and magazines and then pasting each on a card for the word wallet (from an envelope);
- collecting names of animals, foods, toys, friends, relatives, or fun things to do, and more.

Provide an enthusiastic environment with activities that require children to rehearse using the letters and letter combinations in different positions in words. Post blank charts with the letter combination written at the top. Leave a writing tool near the chart, as a means of suggesting that the children write a word for the appropriate word group on the chart.

These few sample formats for instruction can be used appropriately for many skills. Combining implicit and explicit instruction with phonemic analysis provides children with a way to discuss sounds of language and to create words. They react to print, and also create that print. They learn from the strategies how to solve decoding problems independently.

> **CAUTION:** Like cutting teeth, children must be ready to understand how to use phonemes to decode and construct words. Readiness precedes learning. Remember, too, that some children can learn phonetically and some cannot (these children will be discussed later in this book).

Back to Assessment

The phonemic skills that early and new readers are usually expected to learn are included in Figures 2-1, 2-2, 2-3, and 2-4. Remember, you can tell if a child has most probably mastered a skill when you've observed or heard the skill used in at least three functional, independent situations. These checklists are not meant to be prescriptive. They are prepared only to supply teachers with an example of how to prepare a list of skills to use for monitoring children's growth.

Children's Self-Monitoring Tool

Self-monitoring—watching and checking oneself—helps children learn how to take charge of their learning. It also helps them understand what they know, and what they need to learn. It is necessary, in environments that respect students, to provide a self-assessment tool, even for phonics. I suggest the following:

1. Have children write on a piece of paper divided into halves, "What I know," and "What I need to learn" about the sounds of language. Talk to a children individually before each is expected to write. Be sure the child as data (the worksheet, game, or other products) in front of her/him so that describing actions is supported with concrete evidence. Once the student's knowledge and needs are expressed orally by him or her, then there is language for self-monitoring in written form. Figure 2-6 illustrates one child's self-monitoring of her knowledge about making words.

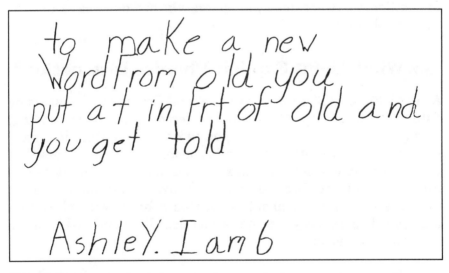

Figure 2-6.

2. Prepare games that provide rehearsal for using phonemic elements. Board games where children are expected to identify

and select the correct blends, word families, and more, are fun. Use the formats of commercial games such as *Monopoly* or *Wheel of Fortune,* for example, to create these.

There continues to be much controversy over explicit instruction with specific sounds of our language. I find, for example, that consensus is never achieved during professional discussions about how or if to teach single and double vowel sounds. Although double vowel sounds, especially within words, are almost impossible for most of us to learn, some children can't learn these sounds, or any other sounds of language. Phonics instruction, for these learners, could complicate the use of other word recognition strategies. This is especially true if the children are pushed and struggle with this type of instruction.

The lack of capacity or inability to use phonics to decode occurs for reasons mentioned earlier, but also because our language does not have enough single letters to represent sounds for words. We've had to create combinations of letters to represent the sounds needed. This has made both phonics and spelling difficult for many. In addition, there are some youngsters who just don't have an aptitude for phonics.

So, What About Explicit Phonics Instruction?

As in traffic jams, "proceed with caution." Continuously assess by listening and looking at how children decode words when reading; how they respond to poems, tongue twisters, and other language plays that focus on letter/sound relationships. Read literature that plays with sounds (see Appendix A), and play with sounds as you talk to the children. Use the formats for instruction shared earlier to create lessons. Think about the purposes for knowing about and learning phonics. Ask yourself the questions I've pondered for more than three decades:

- Until what age or stage do children need to use phonics?
- What do I do with the children I've assessed as nonphonic learners?
- What is the difference between phonics and spelling?

What to Do With the Child Who Can't Learn Phonics Either Implicitly or Explicitly

When hearing the sounds and using them to unlock symbolic representatives of these sounds does not work, alternative word recognition strategies must be used. I have found four such strategies to be successful with many children. The first, and most important, is to read, read, and read some more to children of all ages. Read stories, poems, fables, fiction, and nonfiction at a "reading-to-class time" daily. This increases a sensitivity to the sounds of language, word meanings, genres—everything! In addition, try the implicit activities that include: (1) environmental print activities, (2) listening to literature (especially poetry) that includes lots of single and multiple letter combinations, and (3) explicit strategies for remembering words for both reading and writing.

Environmental Print Activities

Opportunities to play with and become aware of phonemic relationships exist all around us. Peter's mom (page 23–25) seized a propitious moment and used a doctor's waiting room for a learning. The interactions also directed Peter to observe the relationship between his name and "p" at the beginning of words in his environments. This helped to bring what Peter already knew to the new information. Teachers in classrooms need to seize moments for explicit instructional sessions. Group lessons make information important, and provide peer support for reluctant learners.

Explicit Activities Using Environmental Print to Teach Phonics

Activity #1.   Conduct an explicit teaching experience focusing on one phonemic element. For example, use Session #1 of the lesson format on page 27 using the letter "f." Be sure to hang the charts developed in the lesson around the classroom. It is also helpful to photocopy an individual replica of the chart for each child.

Activity #2.   Take a walk with your class. Be sure that each child has either a pad, or clipboard with paper, and a writing tool. Whatever the letter of focus may be, say to the children before the trip,

"We are going play a phonics game. First there have to be two teams. So, this half of the class is team _____ (give it an appropriate name). This half is team _____ . We are going to play the game in the school halls." Line the children up inside your classroom. Say, "Now, when I say go, walk QUIETLY around the first floor of the school. Write down the names of all of the things you see that start with the letter **f** like **fish, farm, flat,** and **fox.** The team that writes the most words is the winner."

This second activity is most effective when it follows from the first. It is, in a sense, a combination of sessions 2 and 3 of the phonic lesson format on pages _____.

There are many other activities in which children can "hunt for words" that fit the topic of the lesson. I am sure that after children are "bombarded" with correct responses, select from choices, and finally collect words, they will know the phonemes and the graphemes the letters represent.

Literature for Learning Phonics

Almost every word in Stanley and Janice Berenstain's *The Berenstains' B Book* (1971) begins with the letter "B." The authors' ability to use humor, repeated language, and rhyming formats make this and many of their books delightful, enticing, and alluring, especially for reluctant readers. *Four Famished Foxes and Fosdyke* by Pamela Edwards (1995), an adventure about four "foxy" brothers who make fun of Fosdyke because he likes fried figs, fennel, and French bread, incorporates at least 60 words that begin with the letter **"F."** These and other books, including those in Appendix A, challenge children's thoughts about how language works, and whets their appetite for literature.

Some reluctant readers resist reading anything, especially when they are skill-related materials. Luring, by involving peers, is often necessary with these youngsters. I suggest, therefore, that you label a shelf in your classroom library, "Books for Buddies." Rubberband two copies of at least six different titles, with all the books related to the sounds of language. Introduce the concept, implicitly, by asking a child to be your reading buddy, and together select and then read a book. During a group discussion time, even show-and-tell, you and your buddy share the activity, and retell the content of your paired reading. This models shared reading for the youngsters and other students will follow your lead.

Additional books for developing phonemic awareness while enjoying great literature are included at the end of this book.

Reading wonderful literature that emphasizes letter sounds enhances phonemic awareness. Search for and read children's literature that focuses on the sounds of language to and with children. Notice children's responses to the literature. Notice, too, if they produce their own words following spelling and rhyming patterns used by the authors. Use the assessment tools in Figures 2-1 through 2-5 to determine each student's strength and needs, and record your observations so meaningful instruction can be planned.

Explicit Strategies for Recalling Words for Reading and Writing

I know that some of you believe that explicit phonics instruction is necessary for ALL children. I disagree with the notion. It's like prescribing aspirin for anyone who has a headache. It's unrealistic. I agree with my friends Regie Routman (1996) and Sandra Wilde (1997) that children don't need explicit instruction in phonics, or even spelling. Phonics can be taught and reinforced during shared reading and writing, and assessed and taught during writing times. When phonics is an outgrowth of these activities, the implication is that phonics is naturally part of the reading/writing process. Most children learn phonics tacitly, without realizing it. When tacit learning occurs, children are learning to use phonics, or anything else, because the skills are needed in order to function as a reader or writer.

I often find myself writing ideas in sentences and phrases, and then rewriting them when trying to figure out what I want to write about. I discovered that I write like this in order to figure out what I know. Then, I write lectures, speeches, or articles learning about what I know by writing about it. Kids have ideas in their heads about how words ought to be spelled and written. They get these ideas from immersion into language from the beginning of their lives. They learn it from hearing stories, poems, and conversations. They learn it by observing adults read, talk, and write, and from parental interactions. They incorporate what they know into their memories, using the information to solve language problems in and out of school. They solve code breaking when reading, and that's phonics. If writing is involved, and it surely is, then where does spelling fit in?

Our teachers always use children's writing to glean information about needed phonics instruction. They examine children's spelling and listen to shared oral readings to make decisions concerning instructional needs. They use instructional strategies mentioned earlier and later in this text. We even prepare strategy sheets so children are able to manipulate the phonemes independently. One such sheet was prepared for several children who needed to learn that they could manipulate letters and letter patterns and create many words. Figure 2-7 is an example of one of the many prepared using the same format. The important things about this worksheet include:

- the reason to make "at" pattern words developed because the student spelled "sat" three different ways in her writing (st, set, sot);

- the worksheet is void of written directions because the materials are designed in such a way that the student knows how to proceed;

- the words are presented as a whole unit, the way children read them, and then broken into phonological units.

The more typical worksheet begins with the parts, and expects the child to create the whole word. A frequently seen format looks somewhat like the following:

Make a word. Add the first letter to "at."

c + at = cat

f + at = fat

m + at = _____

r + at = _____

h + at = _____

b + at = _____

			at		
cat	c	+	at	=	cat
fat	f	+	at	=	fat
sat	s	+	at	=	_____
rat	r	+	at	=	_____
hat	__	+	__	=	_____
nat	__	+	__	=	_____
bat	__	+	__	=	_____
mat	__	+	__	=	_____
zat	__	+	__	=	_____

Figure 2-7.   Whole to Part "at" Worksheet

This format, unlike Figure 2-7, includes written directions, and words are built from parts to whole. Although the differences may seem minimal, they are important. Children, who find reading or following written directions confusing, could be hindered by the above word-making activity.

This format can be used with all initial consonants and vowels that say their name. It can be used, too for any word group or family, where a constant exists.

Children, when they learn how to make words, begin to feel in control of manipulating letters and words. The more they learn, the more risks they will take when spelling words for writing. The fact that beginning phonics includes word construction activities indicates that there is a strong relationship between learning and teaching phonics and spelling. The question many teachers ask is, "Where does phonics instruction end, and spelling instruction begin?"

Summary

Not all children need phonics, but all children need to know that letters and combinations of them represent sounds of language. All children are able to learn to manipulate the letters in order to make words, but not all learn this in the same way. Discovering how each child learns to understand how the orthographic (writing) system works to represent sounds comes first. Then guiding children to learn can happen.

Things To Think About

1. Make a list of the activities (lessons) whose content would lend themselves to the Holdaway learning model.
2. Make a list of all of the daily activities in school where implicit phonics instruction would be productive.
3. Make a list of times, student-centered as well as community-centered, when you think explicit phonics instruction would be a functional necessity.

CHAPTER 3

Teaching Spelling

The relationship between phonics and spelling is so strong, that they really ought to be thought of and discussed as integral skills. But, for the purpose of good politics, and public perceptions, phonics and spelling are discussed separately in this book. As my dad would have said, "Suz, you can fool some of the people some of the time, but when you've learned to fool them all, you understand what they're thinking."

What About the Relationship Between Phonics and Spelling?

Children must know something about the spelling (orthographic) system in order to use phonics. They must know that:

- English has twenty-six letters;
- sometimes we use a letter twice—one next to the other—to represent differences in vowel sounds in words (lose and loose, for example).

When I reread, dear educators, what I've just written, and ask myself, "Is there really a difference between spelling and phonics?" conclusions are unclear, confusing, and puzzling. It's like asking, which comes first, the chicken or the egg? I've come to believe that the processes for learning and using phonics and spelling are similar and interchangeable for many children. Charles Read (1975), in his work with preschool writers who used invented spelling,* found that the spellings represented the regular consonant sounds very consistently.

There is a fine line between phonics and spelling. Seven-year-old Tawanda taught me lots about how children think about both. Her mom had informed us that she insisted that her child learn to read the "right" way, with phonics. Tawanda concluded, during a long discussion involving her mother, myself, and her, "I write words the way they sound to me. I just sound them out and know how to spell words. So, I don't have to know phonics."

When Do Children Need to Be Taught Explicit Phonics?

I have observed thousands of beginning readers and writers over the years. When youngsters write phonetically, producing spelling that represents the rational sounds of language, they're demonstrating that they understand sound/symbol relationships. They already know how phonics is used! Some children's spellings reflect knowledge of some letter sounds, and not others. These children attend to the letters whose sounds are familiar. This is indicated by the fact that the specific part of the word that includes the letter(s) makes sense phonically. These children might benefit from direct instruction, and yet they may not. When children's writing and interactions with literature illustrate that they have no sense about how the sounds of letters work to make words, phonics will, most probably, be **in**appropriate. Some children need to learn spelling rules. The fact that spelling rules guide decoding implies that there is a crossover between spelling and phonics. I am not sure, but I'd say that the strategies that follow guide children to make the transition from learning phonics to learning spelling.

---

*The term "invented spelling" is used to describe words spelled without knowledge of the rules that govern the irregular sounds and spelling of our language. Donald Graves, in a private conversation (1997), referred to this as "temporary spelling." Since spelling is developmental, "temporary" is logical.

From Phonics to Spelling

Assessing and Teaching Spelling

Instructional and assessment procedures most often used in schools have infuriated me since the beginning of my career. Poor spelling has often been equated with inadequate writing ability. My own report cards always showed "poor" in spelling. Low grades were aggravated by a high school teacher's comment, "Susan, you should not pursue a college career. You can't write." Supportive parents' and friends' encouragements were stronger than the recurring teacher's remark in my mind, and I made it through.

Hundreds of thousands of students suffer from the same fate. This happens, I believe, because of (1) the over-emphasis on the importance of spelling, (2) the reasons for spelling problems, (3) a lack of knowledge concerning reasons for failure, and (4) inappropriate instruction and assessment procedures.

How Important Is Spelling?

Spelling is very important. Knowing how to spell enables authors to write quickly, easily, and correctly. It is not as important, however, during initial writing efforts. Before the advent of computers, good handwriting habits were necessary elements in the writing process. Poor spelling habits often resulted and were equated with poor handwriting habits. In today's sophisticated computer age, one is no longer required to struggle to perfect handwriting. The importance of handwriting to the spelling process, therefore, is minimal. The importance it had when students were creating written text has been replaced by expectations that quality writing be produced.

Reasons for Spelling Problems

The nature of spelling, itself, often creates spelling problems. By the time a child begins to spell, she/he has learned to speak and understand the meanings of words. When she learns to spell, she must begin with symbols that make up the word. It isn't sufficient to recognize words as one does when reading. The child must grasp the word in sufficient detail to make it possible for her to reproduce it correctly. It's like recognizing a person when you see her, and paying enough attention to her in order to produce a portrait.

Spelling failures are due, in part, to bad habits that were forced upon children when adults attempted to teach them to spell. This was true of many past practices, and even today some teachers in schools and some parents:

1. continue to use inappropriate instructional strategies, insisting that children who spell incorrectly write, and rewrite the same words again and again;

2. test under timed conditions, and before students have developed automaticity for writing the words;

3. discard or lack knowledge about well-established theories of learning;

4. arouse negative emotions due to assigned, out-of-context word-learning expectations, and then treat the child in uncomfortable ways because of failures.

Strategies and Circumstances That Often Produce Poor Spellers

There is no better way to produce poor spelling habits than to dictate prescribed spelling words to children. Students are asked to study these dictated words usually as homework. More often than not, they are not provided with strategies that guide them to learn the words. Many teachers tell children to memorize, without saying how. Others tell children to use flash cards and don't say how or why. Testing their ability to spell words generally comes once a week. Children who have difficulty spelling words out of context in particular, or who have difficulty due to time constraints often panic, get confused, and can't help but misspell words. Attempts to correct misspelled words often fail. Some classroom teachers even prohibit correcting words during testing. These insensitive teachers move on to the next word, the child begins to write the word late, becomes confused, gets it wrong, knows he's wrong, and the nightmare continues.

The teacher corrects the child's paper by marking the misspelled words in ways that draw the child's attention to misspellings, rather than to correct spellings. This devastating horror is often topped with a poor grade that convinces the child that he is stupid. Handing back the paper enhances poor self-esteem, especially when the student is told to write and rewrite the words correctly a given number of times.

If that's not enough, some teachers require that children stay after the regular school hours to write and rewrite the words. Sometimes a note is sent home, which results in anything from a parent offering a prayer that this "dummy" might learn how to spell, to a severe or even violent punishment.

This monotonous, repetitious writing, and rewriting, causes poor attention. Students become disinterested in the meanings of words because of the boring and sometimes hypnotic nature of repetition. They often withdraw rather than continue to suffer when teachers use their errors as the basis for class discussion and instruction. Try and write your own name between 25 and 100 times and reflect on your feelings. I bet that even your own name becomes a bunch of meaningless symbols. One youngster shared his strategy. "You know what, Susan," he commented, "when my teacher asks me to write a word 25 times, I write the first two letters 25 times, and then the next two letters 25 times, and the last letters 25 times, and it's not so boring." Unfortunately, all this outrageous activity occurs without ever providing students with strategies for learning how to spell and recall the words. They aren't learning HOW to spell and remember words. What they're really learning is that spelling is a boring, tedious, unpleasant, frustrating exercise.

Spelling Techniques Often Used

Teachers usually select one technique for ALL students. The activities generally ask students to: (1) form images in the mind, (2) learn from oral spelling, and (3) copy words. When any single strategy for learning is forced on an entire class of children, some will fail to learn.

Visual Images and Memory

Students with an aptitude for spelling generally picture words in their minds. Poor spellers seem to be unable to use their visual memory effectively to do this. The images they produce are vague and indistinct, preventing them from receiving the details necessary to reproduce the word. Some learners are unable to form any image. There are some who can recall a bit of the word's image, at first. They visualize the rest of the word with rehearsal, over time.

Students who are unable to develop visual images absolutely cannot use visual imagery to learn to spell. They generally respond to auditory stimuli (hearing sounds of the word) and kinesthetic stimuli (using hands, tongue, throat, lip, or eye movements), which takes the place of visual learning. The student needs to feel himself say the word, think the sound, and feel the movements his hand makes when writing the word. It's a commonly used practice to say, "Boys and girls, close your eyes and try to make a picture in your mind of the word." Children who can't "get the image" cannot produce the right answer with this "picture in the mind" approach.

Oral Spelling

Nonvisual learners also have difficulty spelling words one letter at a time. The image of the word as a whole unit is lost as they concentrate on a one-letter image. When they begin to spell the word, they attend to the "letter of the moment," losing all idea of the word itself. These same children have difficulty finding words in a dictionary. Focusing on finding the word by looking at the first letters helps them forget how to pronounce the rest of the word. The usual practice for helping the hard-to-teach, kinesthetic speller has been to spell the word out loud. The ridiculous thing about this is that it's impossible for them to learn this way.

Copying Words

Copying words is discussed in connection with asking students to write words from memory. Children who are auditory-kinesthetic learners have difficulty copying words. The eyes move back and forth from the copy written on paper or a chalkboard at the front of the classroom to the paper. Auditory-kinesthetic learners say each letter as it's copied; they too focus on each letter as a whole, and forget the word.

If hard-to-teach learners with spelling problems are given correct spellings of words each time they need to write them, they will learn how to form the letters. Children who have difficulty spelling, and ask how to spell words when writing, MUST be provided with a written copy of the WHOLE word. Spelling it out, making a picture in their mind, or copying it letter for letter just won't work.

Strategies That (Most Probably) Work

The Modified Ashton-Warner/Fernald Strategy

Grace Fernald (1943) believed that professionals needed to develop ". . . remedial, and preventive techniques that will result in a satisfactory adjustment of the individual to his environment" (p.1). Dr. Fernald supported the idea that students with learning disabilities, developmental lags, and other anomalies needed adjustments in instructional strategies in order to maximize their learning. One of her many techniques designed for students with disabilities in reading and spelling words seems to work for ALL learners. This kinesthetic (type of hands on) approach was first instigated by Plato who lived between 427 and 347 B.C. In discussions concerned with early stages of writing, Plato wrote in the *Protagoras,* "When a boy is not yet clever in writing, the masters first draw lines, and then give him the tablet and make him write as the lines direct." Seneca (3 B.C. to 65 A.D.) suggested that the teacher place his hand on the child's to guide his fingers (Freeman, 1908). Quintillion, a scholar active in the year 68 A.D., recommended, "As soon as the child has begun to know the shapes of the various letters, . . . have them cut as accurately as possible upon a board, so that the pen may be guided along the grooves. Thus mistakes . . . will be rendered impossible, for the pen will be confined between the edges of the letters and will be prevented from going astray." Quintillion advised "learning the sound and the form of the letter simultaneously . . . " (Haarhoff, 1920, pp. 58–59). These philosophers knew, even then, that alternatives were necessary in order for some to learn.

Sylvia Ashton-Warner wrote in *Spinster* (1959) that children don't need "foreign stuff . . . plastered on at all when there's so much inside already. If only I could draw it out. . . . If I had a light enough touch, it would just come out under its own volcanic power" (p. 1). Sylvia found that when she talked to children, she drew out their thoughts, the desire to discuss events, ideas, and things in their lives. As described in *Teacher* (1963), she guided children using the hundreds of words already inside them, thus spurring their desire and comfort to read and write.

I have found in years of working with children and teachers that aspects of Sylvia Ashton-Warner's "key word" approach, coupled with Grace Fernald's methods, are just about foolproof for learning to recognize and write* words. My staff and children in our Center have named our version of the method, The Modified Ashton-Warner/Fernald Strategy.

Our melded strategy needs to be taught to children one-to-one when a child asks, "How do you spell a word?" My teachers go to the children's tables, and teach them the strategy because they need it THEN.

Each student needs a legal-size envelope, or a ring holder that can be opened and closed. Words are written on cards, about 3 × 5 inches in size. The word cards are stored in each child's envelope labeled, "Katie's Words," or on the ring holder with holes punched in one corner. Older children like to file their word cards alphabetically, or by content, or even based on where they were used. Many prefer to write the words in a notebook designated for that pur‚ pose. Use this technique when:

- children find a special word associated with content, discussions, etc.;
- children ask to spell a word needed for their writing;
- several pieces of their text, written independently, indicate instruction.

Katie learned to use this technique in the Center after her teacher realized that this was more effective than any other for writing words. She often wrote without a care about the correct spelling of words. Other times, she knew that she wanted to share her writing and therefore had to spell correctly so others would be able to read it. "How do you spell elephant?" Katie shouted spontaneously one day while writing about her favorite topic. Her teacher pulled a 3 × 5-inch word card from her pocket and placed it in front of Katie. She wrote "elephant," matching her voice to the flow of her written language and holding onto the sound of the vowels until the next consonant was written. After writing the word, the teacher placed her hand over Katie's writing hand, and holding onto the index

---

*The word "spell" not "write" would normally be used in this context. "Write" implies that the words are whole units, with parts, rather than parts (the letters) forming the whole. "Write" describes what students are actually doing.

finger said, "Katie, say the word and trace it with me." The teacher moved both of their hands together, tracing and saying the word simultaneously. The first few tracings were done this way to guide the child in how to use the procedure. After several times, the teacher said, "Do it again yourself, Katie," as she lifted her hand from the child's. Katie traced the word three times. Her teacher watched to be sure that she was using the procedure correctly. Only when tracing is done from left to right, slowly, and the hand moves over every part of each letter, is this procedure effective. The teacher asked if she thought she could say and write the word without looking at the card. Katie responded affirmatively, and the teacher continued, "Katie, turn the card over so you can't see the word, and write your word on a piece of paper." After Katie wrote the word, the teacher directed her to refer to the word card to check for correctness. Katie forgot to include one letter, so she was directed to say and retrace and try again.

The teacher observed Katie for three weeks to be sure that the strategy was effective for her. If the procedure had not been effective, she would have found another.

Generally, this procedure works with almost everyone. It does not work when tracing and saying are incorrectly executed, or when youngsters have severe emotional or social problems (Fernald, 1943). As places where children can practice their words, you might create columns, one for each child in your classroom, on chalkboards or easel paper posted on the walls. Some children prefer to leave their desks to test writing and saying their words. Be sure to inform children that they need to say and trace, without referring to their cards. Most children are able to learn two to four words daily. They ought to write all the words they have learned, one after the other, without their cards.

Some words are not as power packed as others. Students' interest influences learning, as well. If some words pose learning difficulties, the option of trying again or disposing of that word must be built into the process. When the process for using this strategy becomes part of students' repertoire, words relevant to children's lives will be added by them, and learned.

Children who are able to do so can use their word envelope or word box to learn alphabetizing skills. Categorizing by alphabetizing follows naturally.

Some Cautions   The scientific nature of this strategy requires that it be carried out exactly as described. Teachers must observe to be sure children do the following:

- trace and say the word simultaneously;
- trace and say the word slowly and with care;
- never spell out the word, always say and trace;
- review by tracing, saying, and writing the words, daily.

Although Grace Fernald (1943) and Sylvia Ashton-Warner (1963) developed their techniques for children who had difficulty learning, I, and others, have used it to remember statistical formulas, technical spellings, and more. It works with special needs students, those average, and those considered gifted. It is most effective when children learn words they select because they need them for their writing.

Self-Questioning Strategy

Self-questioning guides students to focus attention on word elements. I've prepared a self-questioning guide sheet that children use independently. With practice, most children remember how to write the word from memory because they've asked themselves these questions. The following strategy sheet should be placed with other spelling strategies for easy access for children of all ages. Again, written directions for using the self-questions are necessary.

What letter begins the word?

What letter ends the word?

What vowels are in the word?

What little words are in the word?

What spelling pattern is in the word?

All of these questions may not be appropriate for remembering all words.

Spelling Workshop Strategy

Imagine looking for a telephone number in a phone book and not having paper to write it on. I get frustrated, but then I say the number, repeating it again and again until I've dialed and reached my party. Repetition and rehearsal are strategies for recall. They are the basis for the Spelling Workshop created for middle- and upper-grade students. The unique part of this strategy is that students are able to move through the workshop independently. All of the strategies for learning to remember how to spell words are present throughout.

We make these available to students as they want to use them. The workshop combines a series of strategies that guide students to learn to write words from memory without teacher intervention (Figure 3-1). It also includes self-testing throughout. Third-grade teacher Katrin Rooman gives each of her children the workshop at the beginning of the school week. She structures the use of the workshop as follows:

> *Monday:*   Student and teacher, together, develop a personal list of words for the week. The words are taken from their Spelling Trend Assessment sheet (Figure 3-2). This assessment tool includes words from content area and writing projects which are misspelled. Once you've collected the misspellings, write the word correctly in the middle column, and then in the last, note the error. If for example, the student spells "her" as "hir," you probably can be certain that a lesson about the "er, ir, ur" spelling rule is appropriate. Direct instruction using the format illustrated for explicit phonics will guide your students to spell correctly. Students feel the need to spell words correctly when they are preparing projects to share. The number of words for each child depends on his/her capacity.

> *Tuesdays, Wednesdays, and Thursdays:*   Children, individually or in pairs, use the spelling workshop as it self-directs. Word games that include at least two, but preferably four players, are wonderful activities for repetition and rehearsal activities. They are "sort of" quizzes monitored by peers.

> *Fridays:*   At the end of the week, Katrin uses a student buddy system for children to self-test. They find a spot congenial for two, and give each other a make-believe spelling quiz in the traditional format. Since each child's words are personalized, the tester is rehearsing reading the peer's words. Peer testing

Spelling Workshop

STEP 1 Read your spelling words. Look at them for a few minutes. Have someone dictate them to you.

_____

_____

_____

STEP 2 Write the words you spelled correctly.

_____

_____

_____

Write the words you misspelled, correctly.

_____

_____

_____

STEP 3 Write your spelling words here.

_____

_____

_____

Write the small words that you see in each spelling word.

_____

_____

_____

STEP 4 Write your spelling words.

_____

_____

_____

Write words that rhyme with your spelling words.

_____

_____

_____

STEP 5 Write your words from memory.

_____

_____

_____

STEP 6 Write the words you spelled correctly.

_____

_____

_____

Write the words you misspelled, correctly.

_____

_____

_____

Figure 3-1. Spelling Workshop (Page 1 of 2)

STEP 7 Find the word card with the correct spellings for misspelled words.

Take ONE word card.

Say the word to yourself or out loud.

Trace the word with your finger saying the word as you trace.

Keep saying and tracing the word until you think you can write it from memory.

Turn the word card over so you can't see it.

Write the word from memory.

Do another word.

Write it from memory.

Do another word.

Write the word from memory.

Trace and say, and write three words correctly.

Take A Break!

After you trace and say and write five words, put all the word cards on the table. Look at them, then...

Make believe you are taking the test. Write these five words from memory.

STEP 8 Give the words you learned to a friend. Ask your friend to dictate the words you learned. Write them here.

_____

_____

STEP 9 Write the words you spelled correctly.

_____

_____

Write the words you misspelled, correctly.

_____

_____

STEP 10 Trace the words you still need to learn. Write them here when you think you can write them from memory.

_____

_____

Figure 3-1.   Spelling Workshop (Page 2 of 2)

is usually game-like, creating a relaxed, nurturing environment for learning.

Katrin conferences briefly with each of the twenty-two children in her classroom during the week, as they work through the activities. She checks for habit building, and spelling errors. Her goal is to find the trends that cause the spelling errors, and teach appropriate strategies.

SPELLING TREND ASSESSMENT

Student's Spelling	Correct Spelling	Patterns Noted
jod	job	reversal of "b"
Trilion	Trenton	phonetic
write	writes	didn't pluralize
frown	from	phonetic -
tocck	tooth	phonetic-
trown	frum	phonetic -
zeez	zebra	initial consonant & vowel sounds
sken	skin	phonetic - vowel sub.
fishs	fish's	possessive rule
beuse	because	initial consonant & vowel sound & ending - missing middle 2 letter blend
to	two	homophone - confusion
dog	dogs	pluralize
form	from	transposed "ro"
happie	happy	phonetic (- y - sound)
frouned	pronounce	initial consonants & vowel sounds
woke	work	phonetic - omission of "r" extra "e"sound
wat	what	phonetic - omission of "h" - wh
repole	report	initial sounds
Satday	Saturday	phonetic
to	too	homophone
borb	board	phonetic - reversal of b for d

Spelling is: Mostly natural (temporary)__✓__   Mostly conventional____

Source(s) of words: unguided writing, retell, reading log, journal, & sentence projective

Instructional Needs: Fernauld technique, encourage to take time when spelling - seems to rush - point out careless errors (missing letters) Explain/model - use of possession & pluralizing words, direct praise for taking risks, continue using word bank/cards, make word cards for words that are repeatedly spelled in a temporary format -

Student's Name: Quaeenkqua Woods   Date: 3/5

Teacher's Name Kristine Kaufman

Figure 3-2. Quaeenkqua's Spelling Trend Assessment

Assessing Spelling

Three things seem to be most important when assessing spelling: (1) today's concept of spelling; (2) spelling development; and (3) characteristics of good spellers.

Today's Concept of Spelling

The last ten years have changed our view of the spelling process. In earlier years, good spellers were students who "mastered" large numbers of words. Sandra Wilde (1992) tells us that today, "children's spelling is not only [considered] a reflection of children's exposure to and knowledge of words but an indication of their understanding of the system of complex and varied patterns" (p. 19). Children learn about how words are spelled and why. The concept of spelling has changed from a static to an active process because we've learned a lot about children's cognitive development as it relates to literacy.

Spelling Development

Children acquire information about our spelling system long before they come to school (Clay, 1975; Gentry, 1987). They discover and experiment with lines, curves, circles, and other forms that make letters. As they play, they learn that (1) print represents talk, and (2) that print also looks the same. We also know by observing very young children that their scribble moves from left to right. This indicates that they've discovered, very early, that writing is horizontal.

When children are able to distinguish characteristics of written forms, they begin to write lines characteristic of letters, and then letters themselves. The discovery that children have made when they write is that there is a system for writing. This is the beginning of spelling development. Gentry and Gillet (1993) divide the development of spelling into five stages, as defined in Figure 3-3.

Characteristics of Good Spellers

Good spellers are able to visualize a word in their minds. They can store the image of the word and access that image when they need to write the word. Most poor spellers are unable to do this. Words that include letters that have different sounds—such as "g"

Stage	Child's Writing	Translation	Age
Precommunicative	SOPLOVS	Says, "It's a story about my sister."	3 years, 3 months.
Semiphonetic (captions or labels)	fon col	phone call	5 years, 11 months.
Phonetic	Lus tok a mos to ski	Luis took a mouse to school.	6 years, 3 months.
Transitional	I won't a fon be cus mi friends hav won.	I want a phone because my friends have one.	7 years.
Conventional	Monday I went to my aunt Nancy. she gave me a kitten.		7 years, 9 months.

Figure 3-3. Spelling Development

in giraffe, which has the sound of "j"—cause much difficulty for these learners. Without a picture in their minds of the word, a "j" would be used at the beginning, for that's the sound one hears.

There is little research explaining why some can and others cannot visualize a word, but it is important to notice the behaviors of children as they write words, and take note of how they produce words. When the letters used replicate only sounds, not irregularities in spellings, students most probably have difficulties with visual imagery.

Children write from the time they are able to hold onto and control a writing tool. Their markings reflect the writing formats of their language and culture. The more children write, the more they learn about the spelling system. It is important, therefore, to keep continuous records of their spelling habits so that you can determine their development and an instructional plan.

Teacher Assessment of Spelling Development

Eight-year-old Quaeenkqua had difficulty spelling. Her teacher decided that she had to focus on her writing for two weeks. This would help her to get a sample of her spellings, so that she could study her spelling habits. Kristine, her teacher, collected the child's spellings of words and recorded them on the "Spelling Trend Assessment" sheet (Figure 3-2). The words were taken from routine writing activities, as well as other written products. The child's spelling trends were summarized so that appropriate instruction could be planned based on Quaeenkqua's needs. The analysis showed that Quaeenkqua spelled words the way they sounded. She seemed to attend to specific sounds within the word, lost attention, and stopped noticing specifics about spelling in the middle of words (i.e., zeez for zebra; pround for pronounce, Satday for Saturday). It was evident that she understood spelling conventions by her use of the double (ee), Zebra (zeez), "tion" in Trenton (Treltion), and "le" in report (repole). Causes for misspellings may be multiple. Some possibilities include (1) an inability to attend to task for more than a few moments, (2) poor memory for visual images of words, or (3) inappropriate or inadequate instruction. The reversed "d" for "b" in Job, and "form" for "from" might indicate some perceptual problems, since Quaeenkqua is more than eight years old. The section labeled "instructional needs" at the bottom of Figure 3-2 provides suggestions for instruction.

Student Self-Assessment of Spelling Development

My goal for students of all ages is to provide them with self-monitoring tools so they are able to discuss their strengths and needs. Most children, with rehearsal, are able to learn to self-assess. Self-assessment involves the ability to look at one's own work, but also to feel confidence about oneself as a learner. It is very difficult for an insecure student to look at and find errors. The first thing, therefore, that teachers need to do is to support student efforts in everything they do in order to build their self-confidence. Direct praise (It's great that you told me you spelled the word wrong.") must be used immediately, when teachers observe children's personal critiques. Praise must come for all self-monitoring, even those nonacademic, social, and physical efforts. Discussion and analyses with children in order to guide them to look at their efforts also helps develop this skill. One of our teachers created the "Spelling Self-Monitoring Sheet" with her children. It has proven to be an important tool for building self-confidence and spelling skills, as well. Children often find their errors and correct them. When they are unable to detect misspellings, instruction is probably needed. Imagine how important a ten-year-old feels when she corrects and points out her own errors (Figure 3-4). Once she is able to describe her needs, she's automatically making corrections. So, assessment is, in fact, the instruction when self-monitoring spelling.

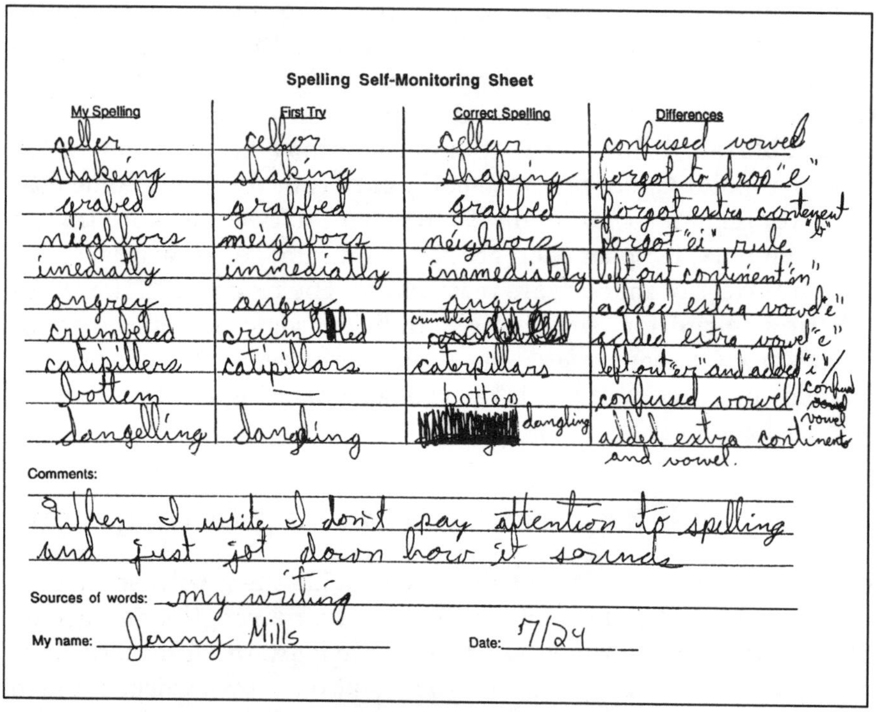

Spelling Self-Monitoring Sheet

My Spelling	First Try	Correct Spelling	Differences
seller	cellor	cellar	confused vowels
shakeing	shaking	shaking	forgot to drop "e"
grabed	grabbed	grabbed	forgot extra constenent "b"
nieghbors	neighbors	neighbors	forgot "ei" rule
imediatly	immediatly	immediately	left out continent "m"
angrey	angry	angry	added extra vowel "e"
crumbeled	crumbled	crumbled	added extra vowel "e"
catipillers	catipillars	caterpillars	left out "er" and added "i" / confused vowel
bottem	—	bottom	confused vowel
dangelling	dangling	dangling	added extra continents and vowel.

Comments: When I write I don't pay attention to spelling and just jot down how it sounds

Sources of words: my writing

My name: Jenny Mills Date: 7/24

Figure 3-4. Jenny's Spelling Self-Monitoring Sheet

Spelling Instruction Driven by Assessment

Danyell discovered from several writing products that Ross continuously misspelled words that included "ir." She developed the worksheets based on the first and second sections of the four-part lesson based on Holdaway's learning model (page 27–30). Her goal was to first bombard Ross with words that included "ir" over and over again, correctly (Figure 3-5). A close look at Ross's work indicates that he attended to the task by going through the story and

---

Name: _____ Date: _____

Write the letters ir in the blanks below to finish this story:

Once there was a girl named Pat who lived in the third house on a long dirt road in Virginia. On the first of April, it would be her thirteenth birthday. Her parents were taking her to the circus to celebrate. When the big day came, she put on her new skirt and shirt. The family traveled for thirty miles to the city. Pat was really enjoying the show, when an elephant began to whirl around and around in a circle. Dust flew everywhere, and Pat was soon covered with dirt. The dirty girl went home. Pat took a bath and soon she was clean again. Pat will remember this birthday even when she is thirty!

Figure 3-5. Ross's "ir" Finish the Story Worksheet

marking the spaces that were to be filled in with "ir." Then he went back and wrote "ir" in the appropriate spaces provided. The second step in the lesson, after bombarding, was to provide Ross with rehearsal space (Figure 3-6). This forced him to review his first efforts, and rewrite the words, focusing on the common element, "ir."

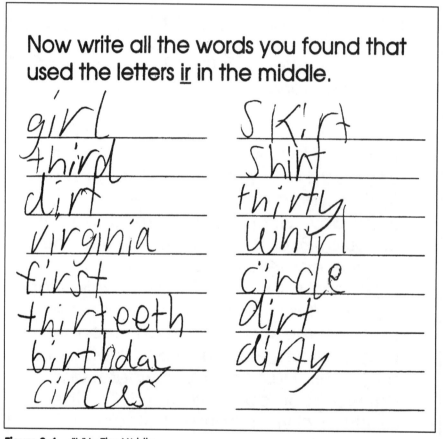

Figure 3-6. "ir" in The Middle

Her third (Figure 3-7) task forced Ross to correctly write "ir" within words. A close examination of Figures 3-5, 3-6, and 3-7 illustrates how even the teaching of phonics needs to be personalized.

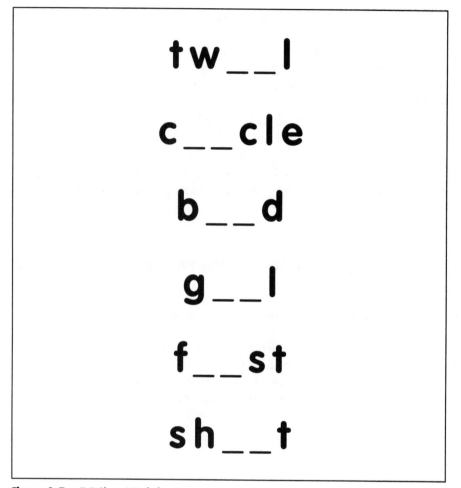

Figure 3-7. "ir" Cloze Worksheet

Spelling instruction is as controversial as phonics. The only relevant way to make spelling meaningful to students is to use students' misspellings found in their written products as the basis for teaching. If you choose to do this, you are making spelling functional by

- teaching, based on student needs;
- making instruction relevant to the student;
- teaching spelling through content area studies.

Summary

Children who can use phonics to learn to decode words are usually able to spell words, during beginning stages of writing, as they sound. The letters and sounds match. Children who find phonics to be difficult or even useless, will probably have a difficult time spelling words correctly, as well. It is our job, as teachers, to find strategies for all children, those who are able to understand sound-symbol relationships and those who are not, how to spell words for writing. What is important is the fact that ALL children need to know what strategy each needs to use in order to remember how to write (spell) words from memory.

Things To Think About

1. If you believe you MUST use a spelling series or a prescribed list of words, what can be done to make the instruction meaningful for each student?
2. Compare the words in the spelling series with those that children request for writing. How many overlap?
3. Focus on one child at a time to observe which spelling strategy is best for guiding that youngster to remember how to spell words.

CHAPTER 4

Word Study, Or Teaching Word Making

The most meaningful and, usually the most fun, is the study of words. Word study combines spelling and meaning. A bit of history (see section of Chapter 1) about the development of language guides students to draw conclusions about how to make words. Knowledge about word origins and groups helps increase students' vocabulary. Knowing that people control aspects of language in order to "make it do something" guides students to love their language, as well. This knowledge also provides them with control over the spelling process. Most important, it expands their vocabulary for reading, writing, and talking.

Expanding Vocabulary

Spelling and phonics is confusing, to say the least. Learning the meanings of words in a logical manner by studying word groups and origins makes the process easier.

How Words Get Their Meanings

American English grew as the result of contributions from many other languages. The names of places and people demonstrate that so well. Twenty-seven of our fifty states—more than half—have names of native American origin (McCrum, Cran, & MacNeil, 1992). These include Arkansas and Dakota, which are the names of tribes. It also includes Mississippi, which means "big river," and Alaska, meaning "mainland." Names of some of our states originated because of confusions. When, for example, the native American chief of the Choctaw people was asked the name of his land, he said "red people," which in his language translated as Oklahoma.

All of our state names and many city names were derived from other languages. Chicago means "the place of strong smells." Several French explorers who found the Moingouena people living at the mouth of a river called the place Riviere des Moingouenas. The name des Moines (the monks) eventually evolved. Other places, like New Mexico, New Hampshire, New Jersey, and New York were named by the British who remembered a place in England that resembled the new lands.

Hackensack and Hoboken, as well as Brooklyn and Harlem, take their names from the Dutch. Philadelphia is derived from classical and biblical lore and means "city of brotherly love." The town names King of Prussia, Blue Balls, and Intercourse are derived from tales of the frontier and are still being used today (McCrum, Cran, & MacNeil, 1992).

Using Word Origin Information in Language Study

I suggest that you begin with third graders and up, and with younger children who seem to be able to make connections between derivations and words. Post a list somewhere in the classroom similar to the one below.

Words Created from People's Names

Adam's apple—Adam, the first man, ate the forbidden fruit, an apple.

cardigan—Earl of Cardigan, a British officer whose soldiers wore knitted sweaters.

graham crackers—Sylvester Graham, an American who worked to improve diets for diabetics and vegetarians.

sandwich—John Montagu, Earl of Sandwich, England, who invented the sandwich so he could gamble without stopping to eat a regular meal.

sideburns—Ambrose Burnside, a Civil War general who had thick side whiskers.

teddy bear—named for Teddy Roosevelt, president of the U.S. who spared the life of a bear cub on a hunting trip.

Modify lists to make them age, grade, and interest appropriate for the children you teach. My teachers have begun discussions surrounding derivations of words in other implicit situations. While children were decorating the classroom for a class play based on the storybook, *Reuben Runs Away* (Galbraith, 1987), Lynn began to discuss the derivation of the phrase "teddy bear."

Lynn: This teddy bear looks just like Reuben.

Child: Yeah. And it looks like my teddy bear at home.

Lynn: Do you know how the bear got the name Teddy?

Child: I thought that's what all bears were called.

Lynn: They are now, but they never were before Teddy Roosevelt was president of the United States.

Child: Oh, they named the teddy bear after the president?

Lynn: Yeah, but they did it because when he was on a hunting trip, he refused to shoot a baby bear. So, he saved all baby bear cubs, and after that baby bear toys were all called teddy bears, after the president's name "Teddy."

Child: So, teddy bears are named after a president.

Lynn: Yep. And Adam's apple, you know that bump that is right here (points to her throat) in a man's neck. Well, it's named after Adam, the first man on the earth. He ate the apple, and the lump in his neck is part of the apple that was supposed to have gotten stuck in his throat. Adam's Apple. It is the lump that sticks out. Other objects get their names from other things. I could call the mobile that you made for your science project, Sophia, a Sophia Mobile.

Child: Cause Sophia is my name and I made it?

Lynn: You're right! So any mobile that is like yours will always be called a Sophia mobile. Do you know the shot—the vaccine you get so that you don't get polio?

Child: Yeah, I hate shots.

Lynn: Well, it's called the Salk vaccine because Dr. Salk invented it.

Child: I had the German measles. Did a German invent it?

Lynn: I dont know, but I bet somebody in Germany discovered that is was a sickness.

Implicit instruction through casual one-on-one conversation during other activities provokes thoughts about derivations and meaning. It also spurs children to talk about words outside of the classroom. Sophia's grandmother told me that the child insisted that they go through the dictionary to find words that were names. How great it was to discover that the teacher's "teachable moment" guided Sophia in how to explain the process to her grandfather and initiated further investigation of things named for people. The interest was high, the enthusiasm outstanding. Think of how often children create homework and carry it out without it being assigned!

There are many categories of word origins. These include:

- **clipped words**—words that have been shortened or clipped (limo for limousine, exam for examination, bus for omnibus, etc.);

- **portmanteau**—words blended together to make a new one (blot + botch = blotch, flutter + hurry = flurry, smack + mash = smash, twist + whirl = twirl);

- **compounds**—words glued together that sometimes take on a new meaning (back+ yard = backyard, wrist + watch = wrist-watch);

- **contractions**—words where an apostrophe is used in place of one or more letters (I'm for I and am, you'd for you and would, we'll for we and will);

- **acronyms and initializations**—first letters of each word used to represent a name (ABC = American Broadcasting Company, CEO = chief executive officer, DA = district attorney);

- **onomatopoeia**—words borrowed from sounds resembling the real sound that it refers to (arf arf, crash, kerchoo, tap);

- **phobia words**—words derived from the Greek word *phobos,* meaning "fear" (aerophobia means fear of flying, pyrophobia means fear of fire);

- **ology words**—used as a suffix meaning "the science of" (biology means the science of life, criminology means the science of crime).

Knowing the meanings of prefixes, suffixes, and roots helps vocabulary for reading, writing, and oral language to grow. When students know, for example, that the prefix **quadra** means four, they are able to discover the meaning of words including **quadrangle, quadrant, quart,** and **quarter.** The suffix **or,** for example, means "one who." When the meaning of this popular word ending is shared, youngsters easily understand that an actor is *one who* acts, and a donor, *one who* contributes. Teachers with whom I've worked have created exciting and fun ways to guide children to understand concepts these categories generate about words. The following are examples of activities.

Using Interesting Words

I suggest that you select a word category, choose one word daily belonging to that category, and use it in your daily talk. Post the word on a chart labeled "Interesting Word of the Day." You might also want to create a mobile for the category of words, making and hanging one card for each word on the structure.

Ingrid selected the category "phobia" to use for a one-week period of time. She picked five words, using one each day in order to spark interest, and teach the meaning of words functionally. She chose to begin with the word *nyctophobia,* which means "fear of darkness." This seemed timely, for it was the middle of October, and the word fit easily into the Halloween scheme. She used the word as often as possible in daily activities. She used it as soon as they entered the classroom.

"It's so dark outside today, I'm worried about my mother," remarked Ingrid to several students. "Is your mother sick?", asked a child. "No, not really," replied Ingrid. "She has nyctophobia, so when it's dark out like it is today, she gets scared." "Oh," responded another child without further comment or questions. Later in the morning when a child shared her Halloween picture, Ingrid remarked, "Oh my goodness, if my mother were in a house as dark as the one you've drawn, she'd be scared stiff." "Why?" asked the child. "Well," continued Ingrid, "she has nyctophobia. She's afraid of the dark." Ingrid continued to use the word as often as appropriate. She wrote it on the word chart, and also made a card for the mobile that hung from the ceiling. Children will figure out what you are doing after several days, even on the first. One six-year-old said, "You used that word a lot today." This comment indicates that this strategy is working with this child. Ingrid's response, "You are right. I am using the word a lot today. I like the way it sounds, and it is good for today, because it is dark outside. My mother is afraid of the dark, and the word nyctophobia means afraid of the dark," supports the child's attention to her instruction.

I've encouraged children to create their own "phobia" words. Some written by children ages 7 through 12 include:

> assignaphobia—meaning fear of homework
> mediphobia—meaning fear of medicines
> sisaphobia—meaning scared of my little sister
> blindaphobia—meaning fear of a blind date

Modification of this procedure works for guiding children to learn compound words and portmanteau words. Youngsters get excited about gluing words together to form new words. Exhibiting a list of blend-together words, and casually discussing these with children, much as Lynn did with word origins, spurs students to create their own. *The test of understanding is students' own word creations.* Instruction has led children to perform, demonstrating their learning. The following list is a collection of words that were created by children between the ages of six and nine.

> Barbjo = <u>Bar</u>bie dressed in G.I. <u>Jo</u>e's clothing
> mudo = <u>mud</u> that looks like dog <u>do</u> (excretive waste)
> Jupto = a new plant formed from pieces of <u>Jup</u>iter and Plu<u>to</u>
> compable = a t<u>able</u> for a <u>comp</u>uter

Discussions result in word inventions that make language study at times fascinating and at other times, comical.

There are many opportunities to use words from different groups in functional yet natural conversations. Using real and students' created words meaningfully is the most effective way to teach word meaning and their origins. When children use the words in their oral language and writing, and understand how words are created, they've taken and passed the test of understanding.

Using Word Roots to "Decode" Meaning

"My word is *microdermazitz*," shouted fourteen-year-old Stacy. "It's simple. Micro means small, derma means skin, and," pointing to a pimple on her cheek, "this is a zitz. If you put it all together, you've got *microdermazitz*, a small pimple on my skin." Wow! What a wonderful test of comprehension!

The following procedure seems to work for guiding students to understand how roots affect word meanings, and how they help humans create words.

Teacher: Each of these words in my list has something the same. Who sees it

bicycle	bimonthly
bicolor	biennial
bidentrate	bicentennial

Melanie: I do. They all have "bi."

Teacher: Right! They all have "bi" at the beginning. Let's say them together (she points to bicycle first, and moves from left to right as she and the children read them in unison). Now what is a bicycle?

John: It's a two-wheel bike and I have a new one that I got for my birthday.

Teacher: Right, John, it's a bike with two wheels. What about bimonthly?

Joshua: Well, I guess it means two months?

Teacher: Why?

Joshua: Because there is "bi" in the front. And "bi," bicycle was a two-wheeler, so it means two months.

Teacher: Close. The actual meaning is, every two months.

Joshua: Oh, yeah, but it could mean two months, too.

Teacher: You're right, Josh. Very creative! That's how words get meaning; people thinking of meanings of words because of their parts.

Mandy: I know what bicolor means. It means two colors.

Teacher: Cool. You got it. Why does it mean that, Mandy?

Mandy: Because "bi" means two like in bicycle, and it has "bi" at the beginning.

Teacher: And biennial means every two years.

Steven: How did you know that one?

Teacher: Well, "bi" is two, and then I know that annual means every year, so the rest of biennial is like annual, so I just guessed it from those two things.

Steven: Cool! You don't even need a dictionary to find out what it means.

Rachael: I think I know what bidentate means. It could mean two dentists because "dent" is the first part of dentist.

Teacher: Wow! I'm impressed with how you're all discovering out the meanings of these "bi" words.

Kristin: It's easy because of the "bi." All the words mean something about two.

Teacher: What about bicentennial?

Larry: I know what it means. It means something that happens every 200 years.

Teacher: How'd you know that, Larry?

Larry: My grandma had a party when America was 200 years old. My Mom told me about it. It was on her balcony and you can see the water there, and there were all the tall ships, too.

Teacher: So you figured out the meaning of bicentennial because you remember the experience you had at the bicentennial celebration of America.

Larry: Yeah!

Teacher: So, "bi" means (raises her voice waiting for the children to respond)—

Children: Two.

The following words were created by a five- and six-year-old after several discussions similar to the one above.

> Homobono—meaning good man
> homoderma—meaning man's skin
> bihomo—meaning two men

I suggest posting root charts with the root, labeling the chart and a list of words including the root following. You might want to write the meaning of the root at the bottom of the chart AFTER the students discover it. This sort of activity can be done with any Greek or Latin roots.

Word Groups for Meaning Making

The study of word groups is more often seen than other types of language study. These include synonyms, antonyms, analogies, similes, metaphors, idiomatic expressions, word idioms, and also proverbs, and euphemisms. Children's books that use these word groups entice, enhance, and encourage children to understand their concepts (see Appendix A). Teachers have used elements of these groups in creative and whimsical ways so children can learn about them. Board games, especially, are wonderful for guiding students to understand word groups. Basic rules from popular games (including *Password, Monopoly,* and *Scrabble,* for example) provide recreational activities that facilitate learning. Dizzy is a natural for synonyms, antonyms, and analogies.

Using Word Groups in Conversations

One way to guide children to understand that synonyms are words that have similar meanings is to use synonyms in daily conversations as much as possible. Switching from one word to the next several times will guide students to "catch-the-fact" that more than one word means the same thing. The following dialogue between a teacher and a child during a free work and play time illustrates this procedure.

Teacher: Gee, Kim. You're so able with creative writing.

Kim: Yeah, I like to write a lot.

Teacher: I see that. Being capable makes you like it.

Kim: I love to write in my diary the best.

Teacher: That's because you're a competent writer who can write like she talks. When we do something competently, we usually like it.

Assessing Students' Knowledge of Word Groups, Origins, and Expanded Vocabulary

There are several ways students' knowledge can be assessed. The checksheet in Figure 4-1 is one observational guide for determining students' growth and instructional needs.

Student Self-monitoring of Word Knowledge

Using words functionally is the "test" of learning. When students create words using word roots, prefixes, suffixes, and word groups

Word Study Observation Guide

Observed Behaviors

Uses word(s) in the following kinds of conversations

    Uses word(s) for writing.

    _____   _____   _____

    _____   _____   _____

    _____   _____   _____

    Can discover meaning from the word root(s)

    _____   _____   _____

    _____   _____   _____

    _____   _____   _____

    Discovers word meaning from prefix

_____   _____   _____

    Discovers word meaning from suffix

_____   _____   _____

Creates new words using prefixes. The words are

    Word _____, meaning _____

    Word _____, meaning _____

    Word _____, meaning _____

    Word _____, meaning _____

    Word _____, meaning _____

Creates his own words using suffixes. The words are

    Word _____, meaning _____

    Word _____, meaning _____

    Word _____, meaning _____

    Word _____, meaning _____

Figure 4-1.   Word Study Observation Guide (Page 1 of 2)

Creates words using word origins including roots, prefixes, suffixes, and word groups.

Word _____, origin _____

Word _____, origin _____

Word _____, origin _____

Word _____, origin _____

Student knows the following word origins and how to originate her/his own words in each category:

clipped words_____

portmanteau words_____

compound words_____

contractions_____

acronyms and initializations_____

words borrowed from names_____

onomatopoeia _____

phobia words _____

Evidence of student mastery_____

Knows about, and uses in oral language and writing the following word groups:

synonyms_____ metaphors_____

antonyms_____ idiomatic expressions_____

analogies_____ similes_____

Evidence_____

_____

_____

Student talks, spontaneously, about word studies during free time, lunch, playground activities, etc.

Figure 4-1. Word Study Observation Guide (Page 2 of 2)

and families in their creative writing, diaries, and journals, they've demonstrated that they understand the meanings of the parts, and how words are created. Students need to discover that they have incorporated new words and origins in their knowledge base. I suggest the following:

A notebook can serve to catalog new words by organizing those learned (1) alphabetically, (2) into categories based on word origins or groups, or families, and (3) into content area categories, or any other organizational system selected by each student. They might also list new words they've created on a wall chart, or at the back of a notebook. It is best for students to select for themselves their monitoring system. I suggest, however, that all children continue to record their progress.

Summary

The content of this book says that phonics, spelling, and word study are important for reading and writing. Students need to know that there are logical descriptions, definitions, and instructional practices for learning the sounds, spellings, and origins of words. The book promotes teacher assessment practices, and student self-monitoring activities that are integrated into daily classroom activities and content area studies. I hope the content is used to simplify students' understanding of our complicated language. I hope, too, that the book helps you remember that when children learn phonics, spelling, and word studies they are learning skills that are important for all content areas. Without the need to learn content—science, social studies, math, and more—there is really minimal need to learn literacy skills.

APPENDIX A

Literature for Phonics, Spelling, and Word Study

by Phyllis DiMartino Fantauzzo

Phonemic Awareness

Alliteration and Beginning Sounds

A is for angry: An animal and adjective alphabet. (1983). Sandra Boynton. New York: Workman Publishers.

The A to Z beastly jamboree. (1996). Robert Bender. New York: Dutton Children's Books.

Alligator arrived with apples: A potluck alphabet feast. (1987). Crescent Dragonwagon. Jose Aruego & Ariane Dewey (Ills.). New York: Macmillan.

Alligators all around. (1962). Maurice Sendak. New York: Harper.

The amazing animal alphabet book. (1988). Roger & Mariko Chouinard. Roger Chouinard (Ill.). New York: Doubleday & Co.

Animalia. (1986). Graeme Base. New York: Penquin.

Chicka chicka boom boom. (1989). Bill Martin, Jr. & John Archambault. Lois Ehlert (Ill.). New York: Simon & Schuster.

Four famished foxes and Fosdyke. (1995). Pamela Duncan Edwards. Henry Cole (Ill.). New York: Harper Trophy.

Six sleepy sheep. (1991). Jeffie Ross Gardon. John O'Brien (Ill.). Honesdale, PA: Caroline House, an imprint of Boyds Mills Press.

Watch William walk. (1997). Mary Ann Hoberman. Marla Frazee (ill.). New York: Greenwillow.

Word Patterns

The cat in the hat. (1968). Dr. Seuss. New York: Random House.
Green eggs and ham. (1960). Dr. Seuss. New York: Random House.
Jesse Bear, what will you wear. (1986). Nancy White Carlstrom. Bruce Degen (Ill.). New York: Macmillan Publishing.
Mig the pig: A flip-the-page rhyming book (1984). Colin & Jacqui Hawkins. New York: G. P. Putnam's Sons.
Play with "a" and "t." (1989). Jane Belk Moncure. Jodie McCallum (Ill.). Elgin, IL: The Child's World.
Zug the bug: A flip-the-page rhyming book. (1988). Colin & Jacqui Hawkins. New York: G. P. Putnam's Sons.

Rhymes and Ending Sounds

Cowboy bunnies. (1997). Christine Loomis. Ora Eitan (Ill.). New York: Putnam.
The digging-est dog. (1967). Al Perkins. Eric Gurney (Ill.). New York: Random House.
A fish out of water. (1989). Helen Palmer. P.D. Eastman (Ill.). New York: Random House.
I meant to clean my room today. (1988). Miriam Nerlove. New York: Macmillan.
Is your mama a llama? (1989). Deborah Guarino. Steven Kellogg (Ill). New York: Scholastic.
The pillow war. (1998). Matt Novak. New York: Orchard Books.
Round and round again. (1994). Nancy Van Laan. Nadine Bernard Westcott. (Ill.) New York: Hyperion Books for Children.
Sheep in a jeep. (1986) Nancy Shaw. Margot Apple (Ill.). Boston: Houghton Mifflin.
Teddy bear towers. (1991). Bruce Degen. New York: HarperCollins.
"There are rocks in my socks," said the ox to the fox. (1979). Patricia Thomas. Mordicai Gerstein (Ill.). New York: Lothrop, Lee, & Shepard.

Repetitive and Predictable Language

1 hunter (1982). Pat Hutchins. New York: Greenwillow.
Barnyard Song. (1997). Robert Bender. New York: Atheneum Books.
Brown bear, brown bear, what do you see. (1967-1983). Bill Martin, Jr. Eric Carle (Ill.). New York: Henry Holt.

The cat and the fiddle & more. (1992). Jim Aylesworth. Richard Hull (Ill.). New York: Antheneum.

A dark dark tale. (1981). Ruth Brown. New York: Dial.

Five little monkeys. (1989). Eileen Christelow. New York: Clarion.

Five ugly monsters. Ted Arnold. New York: Scholastic.

The gingerbread boy. (1997). Richard Egielski. New York: HarperCollins.

Good night Owl. (1972). Pat Hutchins. New York: Macmillan.

Have you seen my duckling? (1984). Nancy Tafuri. New York: Greenwillow.

I went walking. (1990). Sue Williams. Julie Vivas (Ill.). New York: Harcourt Brace.

Jump frog jump. (1981). Robert Kalan. Byron Barton (Ill.). New York: Greenwillow.

The little old woman who was not afraid of anything. (1986). Linda Williams. Megan Lloyd (Ill.). New York: Harper Trophy.

Old black fly. (1992). Jim Aylesworth. Stephen Gammell (Ill.). New York: Scholastic.

Old Mister Rabbit: An African American folk song. (1996). Robert Bender (Ill.). Orlando, Fl: Harcourt Brace.

Polar bear, polar bear, what do I hear? (1991). Bill Martin, Jr. New York: Henry Holt.

There was an old lady who swallowed a fly. (1997). Simms Taback. New York: Viking.

To market, to market. (1997). Anne Miranda. Janet Stevens (Ill.). San Diego: Harcourt Brace.

Together. (1989). George Ella Lyons. Vera Rosenberry (Ill.). New York: Orchard Books.

Walking through the jungle. (1997). Debbie Harter. New York: Orchard.

Who said boo? (1992). Cass Hollander. Joe Boddy (Ill.). Columbus, OH: Modern Curriculum Press.

Why can't I fly? (1976). Rita Golden Gelman. Jack Kent (Ill.). New York: Scholastic.

Vocabulary, Sounds, and Word Play

Aardvarks disembark! (1990). Ann Jonas. New York: Greenwillow.

A cache of jewels and other collective nouns. (1987). Ruth Heller. New York: Scholastic.

Hurricane City. (1993). Sarah Weeks. James Warhola (Ill.). New York: HarperCollins.

The preposterous rhinoceros or Alvin's beastly birthday. (1994). Robert Bender. New York: Henry Holt.

Up, up, and away: A book about adverbs. (1991). Ruth Heller. New York: Grosset.

The Z was zapped. (1987). Chris Van Allsburg. Boston: Houghton Mifflin.

Onomatopoeia

Do Bunnies talk? (1992). Dayle Ann Dodds. A. Dubanevich (Ill.). New York: HarperCollins.

Ducks like to swim. (1996). Agnes Verboven. Anne Westerduin (Ill.). New York: Orchard.

Night noises. (1989). Mem Fox. Terry Denton (Ill.). New York: Harcourt Brace.

Roar and more. (1956-1990). Karla Kuskin. New York: HarperCollins.

Sing-a-song of popcorn: Every child's book of poems. (1988). Beatrice Schenk Regniers. New York: Scholastic.

We're going on a bear hunt. (1989). Michael Rosen. Helen Oxenbury (Ill.). New York: Macmillan/McElderry.

Similes, Metaphors, Idioms

The dangerous journey of Doctor McPain to make the sick animals better again. (1994). Leon Steinmetz & Gaile Sarma. Krystyna Stasiak (Ill.). Littleton, MA: Sundance.

It figures! Fun figures of speech. (1993). Marvin Terban. Guilio Maestro. (Ill.). New York: Clarion.

Mad as a wet hen! And other funny idioms. (1987). Marvin Terban. Guilio Maestro (Ill.). New York: Houghton Mifflin.

Many luscious lollipops: A book about adjectives. (1989). Ruth Heller. New York: Scholastic.

Quick as a cricket. (1982-1996). Audrey Woods. Don Woods (Ill.). Auburn, ME: Child's Play.

Punching the clock: Funny action idioms. (1990). Marvin Terban. New York: Clarion.

Fiction with Word Play

The adventures of Isabel. (1992). Ogden Nash. James Marshall (Ill.).
  Boston: Joy Street/Little, Brown & Co. (original text 1963).
The alley cat. (1993). Brian J. Heinz. David Christiana (Ill.). New
  York: Delacorte Press.
Amelia Bedelia. (1963-1992). Peggy Parish. Fritz Siebel (Ill.). New
  York: HarperCollins.
Hush! (1997). Minfong Ho. Holly Meade (Ill.). New York: Orchard.
The King's toothache. (1987). Colin West. Anne Dalton (Ill.). New
  York: Harper & Row.
Leon and Albertine. (1997). Christine Davenier. New York: Orchard
  Books.
Sir Cedric Rides Again. (1986). Roy Gerrard. New York: Farrar,
  Straus & Giroux.

Poetry

Bear in mind. (1989). Bobbye S. Goldstein, (Ed). William Pene
  DuBois (Ill.). New York: Viking.
Beast feast. (1994). Douglas Florian. San Diego: Harcourt Brace.
Good rhymes, good times. (1995). Lee Bennett Hopkins. Frane Lessac
  (Ill.). New York: HarperCollins.
A gopher in the garden and other animal poems. (1966-1967). Jack
  Prelutsky. Robert Leydenfrast (Ill.). New York: Macmillan.
Hailstones and halibut bones. (1961-1989). Mary O'Neill. John
  Wallner (Ill.). New York: Doubleday.
Joyful noise: Poems for two voices. (1988). Paul Fleischman. Eric
  Beddows (Ill.). New York: Harper & Row.
The new kid on the block. (1984). Jack Prelutsky. James Stevenson
  (Ill.). New York: Scholastic.
The Random House book of poetry for children. (1983). Jack
  Prelutsky. Arnold Lobel (Ill.). New York: Random House.

Riddles

Easy as pie: A guessing game of sayings. (1985). Marcia & Michael
  Folsom. Jack Kent (Ill.). New York: Clarion Books.
Q is for duck: An alphabet guessing game. (1980). Mary Elting &
  Michael Folsom. Jack Kent (Ill.). New York: Clarion.

Riddle rhymes. (1995). Charles Ghigna. Julia Gorton (Ill.). New York: Hyperion Books for Children.

Ten ridiculous rhymes with flaps. (1993). Jon Agee. New York: Dutton.

Tomorrow's alphabet. (1996). George Shannon. Donald Crews (Ill.). New York: Greenwillow.

What's a frank frank? Tasty homograph riddles (1984). Giulio Maestro. New York: Clarion.

Spelling

Antics. (1992). Cathi Hepworth. New York: G. P. Putnam & Sons.

Busy buzzing bumblebees and other tongue twisters (1982-1992). Joan Sandin. Paul Meisel (Ill.). New York: HarperCollins.

Huggly gets dressed. (1997). Tedd Arnold. New York. Scholastic.

The Krazees. (1997). Sam Swope. Eric Brace (Ill.). New York: Farrar, Straus & Giroux.

Mouse mess. (1997). Linnea Riley. New York: Scholastic.

Snow dance. (1997). Lezlie Evans. Cynthia Jabar (Ill.). Boston: Houghton Mifflin.

Whatley's quest: An alphabet adventure. (1994). Bruce Whatley & Rosie Smith. Bruce Whatley (Ill.). Sydney, Australia: Harper Collins.

Homophones and Figurative Language

Baby buggy: Buggy baby (A word play flap book). (1997). Harriet Ziefert. Richard Brown (Ill.). Boston: Houghton Mifflin.

A chocolate moose for dinner. (1976). Fred Gwynne. New York: Windmill Books and E. P. Dutton & Co.

Eight ate: A feast of homonym riddles. (1982). Marvin Terban. Giulio Maestro (Ill.). New York: Clarion.

Hey, hay!: A wagonful of funny homonym riddles. (1991). New York: Clarion.

The king who rained. Fred Gwynne. New York: Prentice Hall.

What in the world is a homophone? (1996). Leslie Presson. JoEllen Bosson (Ill.). Hauppauge, NY: Barron's Educational Series.

APPENDIX B

Behavioral Characteristics Indicative of Reading, Writing, or Speaking Problems*

Checklist of Characteristics

Children who have learning difficulties frequently show some combination of the following characteristics.

Reading

____ holds book too close
____ calls words
____ always sounds out words
____ always points to words
____ reverses words (saw = was)
____ sees double
____ re-reads lines (involuntarily)
____ oral reading is choppy
____ always vocalizes during reading
____ cannot tell about what he reads
____ skips lines without knowing it while reading
____ omits ending consonants in oral reading
____ can make little sense of sound-symbol relationships, therefore . . .
____ lacks the ability to use word attack skills

---

*REMEMBER: Some of these characteristics are present in all of us. But students with problems will exhibit many of them. There will be many overlaps, as well. If a child has an excessive number of characteristics, you MUST seek appropriate, special services. *Children with severe problems produce products that are significantly different from those of others in class. Their excessive **inability to remember** stands out from the others.*

____ eyes regress frequently during reading
____ moves head when reading
____ loses place during reading
____ eyes burn or itch
____ frowns and looks sad during reading activities
____ blinks eyes excessively
____ closes or covers one eye during reading
____ squints
____ rubs eyes a lot
____ has difficulty focusing
____ indicates difficulty reading (i.e., "I mess up when I read.")
____ changes syntax ("He always goes." to "He be going.")
____ uses pronouns inappropriately ("Her is here.")

Auditory

____ seems listless
____ frequent colds, allergies, asthma
____ seems to depend on others visually
____ responds to directions slowly
____ difficulty pronouncing words accurately
____ breathes through the mouth
____ has or complains of ear problems
____ complains of dizziness in the head
____ unnatural pitch of voice
____ blank facial expression when speaking to another
____ watches speaker closely
____ uses loud voice
____ needs excessive volume for listening to T.V., radio, VCR, etc.
____ can follow ONLY one direction at a time

Writing

____ inconsistent spacing between words
____ moves body while writing
____ reverses letters
____ produces pressure points in writing
____ has poor posture when writing most of the time
____ writing appears rigid
____ letters vary in size
____ writes short pieces for short periods
____ grips writing tool tightly
____ mixes capital and small letters
____ moves paper while writing
____ letters extend beyond the lines
____ does not follow margins

Spelling

____ omits letters at the beginning and/or end of words
____ omits letters within words
____ can sometimes spell better orally than in writing
____ spells word as if it sounds differently
____ reverses letters
____ transposes letters in words
____ drops letters as people do when talking
____ confuses consonant sounds

Work and Other Habits

____ difficulty getting organized
____ has trouble getting started
____ has many projects going on at the same time; has difficulty following through
____ says what's on his mind without considering its appropriateness
____ searches for high stimulation
____ easily distracted
____ does not tolerate a lack of activity and feels bored
____ often creative, intuitive, and highly intelligent
____ trouble following "proper" procedures
____ impatient; low tolerance for frustration
____ impulsive verbally or actively (changes plans, spends money impulsively, etc.)
____ tends to worry needlessly, endlessly
____ switches moods suddenly
____ is extremely restless
____ older children have tendency toward addictive behaviors

Personality and Physical Characteristics

____ has sense of underachievement, of not meeting goals (even if he does)
____ has difficulty making and keeping friends
____ has sense of insecurity
____ will not (can't) conform
____ moves about a lot
____ difficulty exchanging conversations
____ talks "at" rather than with peers
____ seems uncooperative
____ seems lazy
____ seems careless
____ often bumps into furniture or other large objects
____ is referred to as clumsy

Communication Handicapped

A child who has difficulty understanding language has a RECEP-TIVE language handicap. The child has MANY (not few) of these characteristics.

____ responds inconsistently to sounds or speech
____ has short attention for listening
____ sometimes looks "blank" when spoken to
____ seems frustrated during class discussions
____ has difficulty understanding abstract language
____ has problems with multiple word meanings
____ has difficulty recognizing relationships of words to concepts
____ distracted from speech and seems to listen to environmental sounds
____ has difficulty using phonics as a method of word recognition
____ often gives inappropriate answers (e.g. "What did you do yesterday?" Response might be, "It is warm outside.")
____ has difficulty learning new vocabulary
____ lacks understanding of riddles, jokes, rhymes, or absurdities
____ seems to have a poor memory for what happened during listening activities
____ has difficulty sequencing events (days of week, numbers, story episodes)
____ often repeats a question or statement rather than responding
____ makes impulsive, immediate, inappropriate responses to questions
____ has a tendency to "shadow" questions or directions (subvocally or vocally)

EXPRESSIVE language difficulties result in the child having difficulties organizing thoughts when speaking and writing. The child has some or many of the following characteristics.

____ seems unusually quiet
____ does not contribute to class discussions
____ sometimes uses words incorrectly
____ sometimes uses words in incorrect order in sentences
____ seems lethargic and unanimated
____ uses more physical rather than verbal expression
____ sometimes substitutes one word for another within a category (i.e., orange for apple)
____ has difficulty finding correct describing words (i.e., "You know, that thing we saw?")
____ uses short sentences most of the time
____ rambles on to answer a question or when telling a story or event
____ uses an inordinate amount of "ums," pauses, or repetitions
____ overuses concrete vocabulary
____ seems to be an excessive talker
____ seems hyperverbal
____ often fails to recognize social cues to stop talking

APPENDIX C

Game and Activity Formats for Spelling, Phonics, and Word Study

There's nothing like a game to get children involved, immersed, even "hooked" on phonics, spelling, and word study. The social interactions, peer support, and competition provided by game-like materials spur interest and excite emotions.

Below are several game formats that can be adapted to many phonics, spelling, and word study concepts. Use these as examples to create, and have children create games for learning and reviewing skills, and for just plain old fun.

Phonics, Spelling, and Word Study Game and Activity Formats

Learning how words are made is important for beginning readers. Games whose formats insist upon word making improve students' abilities to decode when reading. The following require that students make words by combining letters at the beginning, with phonograms. Phonograms are usually made with one vowel sound plus a consonant sound (ag, ade, um, it, etc.). Each one can be less than a syllable and, therefore, not a word. To make words each phonogram needs an initial consonant or blend (tag, fade, drum, sit, etc.). Phonograms are wonderful for (1) rhyming and (2) enticing reluctant learners into successful reading and spelling activities. Using rhyming to change the "turned-off" learner into a reader is nothing new. The colonists in the beginning days of our country, teachers, and parents have used rhymes to make language interesting, fun, and predictable.

The following game formats can be adapted for developing many phonics, spelling, and word study skills. These include (1) making words and sometimes deciding what they mean, (2) matching sounds, and (3) selecting words or meanings of words.

1. The Wheel for Making Words Activity (Figure C-1)

Materials: Two circles cut from tag board about the size of a paper plate or paper plates, one circle cut two inches smaller than the other.
One paper fastener
Black or blue marking pen.

Directions for Making: Place the smaller circle in the middle and on top of the larger one. Using the paper fastener, connect both in the center. Write ONE phoneme on the two-inch overlapping space of the larger circle. Write initial consonants, consonant blends, or digraphs equally spaced on the inner circle.

Directions for Using: Have student turn the inner circle so that one letter at a time lines up with the phonogram. Say the word with the child. Then, have the student say it alone. After he says it, have him write it on a piece of paper, and again on a word card (four by six inches). The word cards can be accumulated and stored in an envelope labeled, "(Child's name) Words." They can be reviewed daily independently with a peer partner. Keep the word-making wheels in a central location in the classroom so that children can take these at leisure and work with wheel, independently.

Modifications for Spelling: Write the spelling patterns which a student needs to review on the outside, larger circle, and make and play as described above. This activity is effective with all regularly spelled patterns (at, et, ight, etc.).

Modification for Word Study: Use the smaller circle for a prefix and the outer for different endings that make words using the prefix. Do the same when studying suffixes. This time, however, the outer circle includes only one suffix. The smaller, inner circle includes beginnings that, when combined with the suffix, make words (Figure C-2).

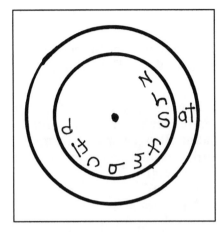

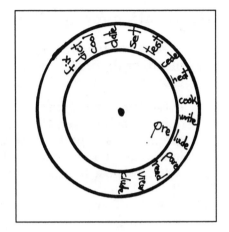

Figure C-1.   **Figure C-1.**

2. Matching Games and Activities

    Materials: One package of four by six inch index cards

    Blue or black marker for writing.

    Directions for Making: Write pairs of phonograms, one per
    card, that rhyme. You might, for example, write "cat" on one
    card and "fat" on a second. Make as many pairs of rhyming
    phonograms as you think the children are able to match in
    one game. No more than twenty are suggested. A few of the
    many phonograms available for this game include: ag, ain, am,
    an, ez, eem, ed, eck, ied, ie, im, ing, obe, ome, old, ool, ort, ow,
    ud, ump, us, ut.

    Directions for Playing the Game: Shuffle the cards. Deal them
    to the players. At least two, but no more than four players are
    suggested. Players pick all of their cards up at one time and
    each holds their cards so they can't be seen by other players.
    All players pull out of their hands the cards that match (two
    with the same word on each). Player #1 begins by asking for a
    card to match one she has in her hand. Players 2, 3, and 4 each
    have one turn. Only one match is made during each player's
    turn. Turns rotate until all of the cards are gone. The player
    with the most matches is the winner. This game tests the
    student's ability to "hear" and match sounds.

Modification for Spelling

Directions for Making: Write the consonants, consonant blend, or digraph, one each per card. Write the same phonogram on two cards (i.e. at).

Directions for Playing: Place the phonogram cards, face up, one for each player. Deal consonant, consonant blend, and digraph cards to players. Each makes REAL words with initial letters dealt and writes each word on a piece of paper. The one with the most REAL words is the winner.

3.   Selecting Games and Activities (A testing activity)

This game format can be auditory (the child listens to select) or visual (the child reads to select). Students who select correctly when they listen, ought to be playing auditory games. Those who seem to be able to use phonics best when reading, should be selecting elements visually.

Phonics and Selecting

Materials: A package of four by six inch index cards.
Blue or black marker.

Directions for Making: Select one phonogram (i.e., at, ing, etc.), family ending (i.e. ology), or suffix (i.e. ism, able, etc.). Write the selected element again and again, one each per card. Write the phonogram again at the top of a large piece of paper, as if preparing to make a list, and underline it. Write initial consonants, consonant blends, or digraphs, one on each card.

Directions for Playing: Deal all cards to two to four players. Pile the multiple copies of the phonogram, word family, or suffix one on top of the other, and place them in the middle of the playing area (table or floor). Each student is dealt the cards with the initial letters on them. In turn, each takes one card from the deck, and makes a word, matching the initial letter(s) with the phonogram, word family, or suffix. After matching, the student writes the word on the chart with his/her initials next to it. The child with the most REAL words after the cards are gone wins.

Modification for Word Meaning

Directions for Playing: Prepare game as directed above; write the phonogram, word, family, or suffix on the top of a large piece of, this time, one sheet for each child. Post it so that the child can easily write on it. Carry out the game as directed above. The child write words on their own chart (Figure C-3). After the game is over, each attempts to define each word. Explanation, telling, "why" words are defined as they are, should be requested. Ask, for example, if the student writes 'catology,' "What does it mean?" Student ought to respond, "The study of cats." Then ask, "Explain why it means study of cats." The student ought to respond, "Ology means "the study of" something. I wrote cats so it is the study of cats."

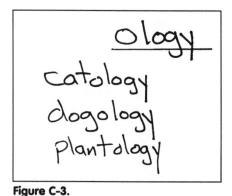

Figure C-3.

Additional Suggestions

Many of the good books mentioned in Appendix A are wonderful resources for creating games. You might, for example, make a matching card game using synonyms. All cards would be dealt and student might, for example, ask for a "synonym for the word cold." If another player had 'freezing,' she would be obligated to give it to the asker. The one with the most matches wins.

Cautions: Remember, games are to reinforcement, review, and relax. If used for anything else, their purposes are lost. Make as many games as you need so children can have the opportunity to identify (select), create, and define letter sounds, and how to use them and their meanings.

REFERENCES

Adams, M. J. (1991). *Beginning to read: Thinking and learning about print.* Cambridge, MA: MIT Press.

Anderson, R. C., Hiebert, E. H., Scott, J. A., & Wilkinson, I. A. G. (1985). *Becoming a national of readers.* Champaign, IL: University of Illinois, Center for the Study of Reading.

Ashton-Warner, S. (1959). *Spinster.* New York: Simon & Schuster.

Ashton-Warner, S. (1963). *Teacher.* New York: Bantam.

Baugh, J. (1983). *Black street speech: Its history, structure, and survival.* Austin, TX: University of Texas Press.

Becker, W. C., & Gerstein, R. (1982). A follow-up of follow through: The later effects of the direct instruction model on children in fifth and sixth grades. *American Educational Research Journal, 19,* 75–92.

Bond, G. L., & Dykstra, R. (1967). The cooperative research program in first-grade reading instruction. *Reading Research Quarterly, 4,* 5–142.

Clay, M. (1975). *What did I write?* Auckland, New Zealand: Heinemann Educational Books.

Fernald, G. M. (1943). *Remedial techniques in basic school subjects.* New York: McGraw-Hill.

Freeman, K. J. (1908). *Schools of Hellas.* London: Macmillan & Company.

Fry, E., Kress, J., & Fountoukidis, D. (Eds.). (1993). *The reading teachers book of list.* New York: The Center for Applied Research.

Gentry, R. (1987). *Spel . . . is a four-letter word.* New York: Scholastic.

Gentry, R., & Gillet, J. W. (1993). *Teaching kids to spell.* Portsmouth, NH: Heinemann.

Glazer, S. M. (1992). *Reading comprehension: Self-monitoring strategies to develop independent readers.* New York: Scholastic.

Glazer, S. M. (1994, March). Self-monitoring: Taking control as a writer. *Teaching, K–8,* 91–92.

Glazer, S. M. (1998). *Children's perceptions about reading and writing the first day of school, 1980–1997.* Unpublished manuscript.

Glazer, S. M., & Brown, C. S., (1993). *Portfolios and beyond: Collaborative assessment in reading and writing.* Norwood, MA: Christopher-Gordon.

Glazer, S. M. & Burke, E. M., (1994). *An integrated approach to early literacy: Literature to language.* Boston: Allyn & Bacon.

Glazer, S. M. & Fantauzzo, P. D., (1993). *Students' understanding of the reading process and perceptions of themselves as readers.* Unpublished manuscript.

Glazer, S. M., & Searfoss, L. W. (1988). *Reading diagnosis and instruction: A C-A-L-M approach.* Englewood Cliffs, NJ: Prentice-Hall.

Haarhoff, T. (1920). *Schools of Gaul.* New York: Oxford University Press.

Henderson, E. (1985). *Teaching spelling.* Boston, MA: Houghton Mifflin.

Holdaway, D. (1979). *The foundations of literacy.* Exeter, NH: Heinemann.

McCrum, R., Cran, W., & MacNeil, R. (1992). *The story of English.* London: BBC Books.

Moffett, J., & Wagner, B. J. (1992). *Student-centered language arts, K–12* (4th ed.). Portsmouth, NH: Heinemann.

Perfetti, C. A. (1992). The representation problem in reading acquisition. In P. B. Gough, L. C. Ehri, & R. Treiman (Eds.), *Reading acquisition* (pp. 145–174). Hillsdale, NJ: Erlbaum.

Perfetti, C. A., & Zhang, S. (1996). What it means to learn to read. In M. F. Graves, P. Van Den Broek, & B. M. Taylor (Eds.), *The first R: Every child's right to read* (pp. 37–61). New York: Teachers College.

Read, C. (1975). *Children's categorizations of speech sounds in English.* Urbana, IL: National Council of Teachers of English.

Routman, R. (1996). *Literacy at the crossroads: Critical talk about reading, writing, and other teaching dilemmas.* Portsmouth, NH: Heinemann.

Smith, F. (1995). *Between hope and havoc: Essays into human learning and education.* Portsmouth, NH: Heinemann.

Tannenhaus, M. K., Flanigan, H., & Seidenberg, M. S. (1980). Orthographic and phonological code activation in auditory and visual word recognition. *Memory and Cognition, 8,* 513–520.

Wilde, S. (1992). *You kan red this! Spellng and punctuation for whole language classrooms, K–6.* Portsmouth, NH: Heinemann.

Wilde, S. (1997). *What's a schwa sound anyway?* Portsmouth, NH: Heinemann.

About the Author

Susan Mandel Glazer is director of the Reading and Writing Center and Professor of Education at Rider University. A past President of the International Reading Association, she is the 1998 recipient of the IRA Outstanding Teacher Educator in Reading Award. She is the author of numerous articles and books, among them *Portfolios and Beyond: Collaborative Assessment in Reading and Writing,* also published by Christopher-Gordon Publishers. A popular presenter, Dr. Glazer is also a Teaching Editor for *Teaching Pre K–8*. She received her Ed.D. from the University of Pennsylvania.

Author Index

Subject Index